Water Dragons

Complete Herp Care

D1370421

Bert Langerwerf

For my wife, Hester, my most inspiring supporter.

Water Dragons

Project Team
Editor: Thomas Mazorlig
Copy Editor: Mary Grangeia
Cover Design: Mary Ann Kahn
Interior Design: Mary Ann Kahn

T.F.H. Publications
President/CEO: Glen S. Axelrod
Executive Vice President: Mark E. Johnson
Publisher: Christopher T. Reggio
Production Manager: Kathy Bontz

T.F.H. Publications, Inc.
One TFH Plaza
Third and Union Avenues
Neptune City, NJ 07753

Printed and bound in China,

06 07 08 09 10   1 3 5 7 9 8 6 4 2

Library of Congress Cataloging-in-Publication Data
Langerwerf, Bert.
Water dragons : a complete guide to Physignathus and more / Bert Langerwerf.
p. cm.
Includes bibliographical references (p.   ) and index.
ISBN 0-7938-2884-8 (alk. paper)
1. Water dragons (Reptiles) as pets. I. Title.
SF459.L5L36 2006
639.3'954--dc22
2005035527

The Leader In Responsible Animal Care For Over 50 Years!™
www.tfhpublications.com

Table of Contents

Introduction _ 4

Chapter 1
Purchasing Your Water Dragon_ _ _ _ _ _ _ _ _ _ _ _ _ _ _ _ _ 8

Chapter 2
Housing _ 18

Chapter 3
Feeding and Nutrition _ 38

Chapter 4
Health Care _ 50

Chapter 5
Green Water Dragons _ 58

Chapter 6
Australian Water Dragons _ _ _ _ _ _ _ _ _ _ _ _ _ _ _ _ _ 78

Chapter 7
Similar Species _ 94

References _ 118

Resources _ 123

Index _ 125

Introduction

Water dragons have been kept as terrarium lizards for a long time. In his famous books on terrarium science, Dr. W. Klingelhöffer (1957) mentions the years 1907, 1908, 1912, and 1913 as years when Australian water dragons may have first been kept as pets. At that time, it was easier to get lizards from Australia than from Indochina. If we look in the book entitled Reptiles and Amphibians From Foreign Countries, written by Dr. K. Floricke in 1912 (in German), we can read what Dr. Klingerhöffer wrote about these lizards to his colleague: The following original German text, which I will also translate, shows how Dr. Klingelhöffer was charmed by these animals almost 100 years ago:

"Wenn sie mit aufgerichteten Vorderbeinen auf einem Ast sass, war ihr Anblick geradezu ein ästhetischer Genuss, so schön war der Schwung ihrer Rückenlinie mit dem gezackten Hautkamm, so harmonisch die im lang herabhängeden Schweife endigende Gestalt." ("When she was sitting with erected front legs on a branch, it was such an esthetical pleasure to look at her, so beautiful was the vault of her back line with the serrated skin crest, so harmonic was the shape of her body ending in a long downward hanging tail").

That must have been before 1912. The charms of the (Australian) water dragon were already known by terrarium keepers of that time. In the period before World War I, Australian water dragons were already being imported to Germany as pets, which indicates that they have been kept as terrarium lizards for almost a century. During that time, a lot has been written about them, initially in German.

During the late 1950s and early 1960s, when I was a teenager, the well-written German books on the subject of keeping terrariums by Dr. Klingelhöffer taught me how to care for and eventually breed these magnificent lizards. Because I wanted to read everything he wrote, I was forced to learn German very early in my life (Dutch is my native language).

Years later, Australia stopped allowing wildlife to be exported. At that time, the captive breeding of this species was unknown territory. I am very pleased that I can bring the

Scientific Names

You may have noticed that sometimes there are words in italics that appear after the name of an animal. This is the scientific name, and each animal only has one scientific name. Biologists determine the scientific name of each animal based on what other animals it is related to. Each scientific name has two parts: The first part of the name is called the genus, while the second part is the species. This combination of genus and species is unique for each animal. Scientific names allow scientists all over the world to talk about each animal without worrying about language barriers or other similar animals being confused with the one they want to discuss.

A scientific name is often abbreviated after the first usage. The genus is abbreviated to the first letter. So, after introducing the green water dragon as *Physignathus cocincinus*, it can be referred to as *P. cocincinus*. If the author is talking about all the lizards in this genus, he or she can use *Physignathus* without a species name attached. Some animals have a third name, which indicates that it is a subspecies. Subspecies describe different varieties that exist within a species.

charms of keeping these animals back to interested terrarium keepers. Since 1992, I have bred water dragons in great quantity.

In this book, I attempt to impart the century-long knowledge that I have learned from these many experts on the subject of keeping and rearing water dragons. During the last dozen years, I have bred over 17,000. I will describe all you need to know about proper care, as well as covering subjects like building terrariums, the diseases of lizards, breeding feeder insects, and health care. Also, I will present information about other agamid lizards that live in similar wet habitats.

Name Game

This book deals mainly with the two species of the genus *Physignatus* (*phys*= bag; *gnathus*= jaw). The lizards that belong to this genus have a characteristic swelling at both sides of the jaw, which is especially striking in males.

Taxonomy

The two species of *Physignathus* lizards live far from each other as none are found in New Guinea, Indonesia, or the Malayan Peninsula. The genus, as a whole, has Australian affinities and is now classified within the Australian subfamily of Amphibolurinae (Macey et al., 2000). This subfamily is part of the acrodont Agamidae. Acrodont means that these lizards have their teeth in the frontal part of their jaws close together in a ridge. The related family of Iguanidae is pleurodont, which means that their teeth are all planted singly inside the jaw.

The genus *Lophognathus* from Australia, New Guinea, and Southeast Indonesia is the closest related genus, and also belongs to the Amphiolurinae. Until 1980, this genus was part of the genus *Physignathus*. (Moody, 1980). The genus *Hydrosaurus* is now placed in the subfamily Hydrosaurinae and is also part of the Agamidae.

According to the latest theory that explains the presence of the *Physignathus cocincinus* in Asia, it's believed that this species must have arrived on the continent when, in ancient times, an island drifted from Australia and joined with Asia (Macey, 2000).

In his book, Nietzke (1980) mentions two species, *P. mentager* and *P. cocincinus*, which are known today as one species, *P. cocincinus*. The difference between both varieties is found in the number of infralabial scales each has: *P. cocincinus* has six to seven and *P. mentager* has eleven infralabial scales. However, he does not mention the range of both varieties.

Chapter 1

Purchasing Your Water Dragon

For the two species of *Physignathus*, the origin of the lizards currently offered for sale is exactly opposite. Nearly all green water dragons being sold are wild-caught lizards, and nearly all—if not all—Australian water dragons offered for sale are captive bred. Since Australia does not allow the export of wildlife, any wild-caught Australian water dragons would be illegally smuggled animals. Most pet shops do not carry this species and some will have them only around the fall, when most breeders are selling hatchlings. The best period to try to purchase this species is from July through October or early November.

Selecting a Healthy Water Dragon

Almost all water dragons available for sale are babies or are very young animals. When purchasing a water dragon, be sure to examine the animal carefully. A healthy baby must have open eyes and should not look skinny. The tail root should be clean. If some whitish remnants stick to the tail root behind the cloaca (or vent, the opening for elimination and reproductive functions), it means that fat from its food was not digested well, and in most cases, this condition is caused by intestinal parasites such as coccidia, flagellates, etc. If you decide to have a vet check your new purchase and he finds common bacteria, it may not always be wise to treat the animal because these organisms may be normal digestive tract inhabitants. If you keep this in mind, it may not be a bad idea to bring some fresh feces to a vet to check on the condition of your new pet.

Because Australian water dragons are all captive bred and are not cheap to buy, they are usually healthy when offered for sale. As long as the Australian water dragon in question is not thin or displaying some sign of ill health or being kept in inadequate conditions, you should feel confidant that you are buying a healthy pet. Acclimation and quarantine (see below) are still recommended.

Green water dragons are imported world-wide in large numbers, probably hundreds of thousands each year. Most are currently coming out of Vietnam and, therefore, the availability of this species, though high now, can fluctuate. At this time, many people in Vietnam have a low monthly salary, so that it is not very difficult for dealers to purchase high numbers of baby green water dragons from this

The majority of green water dragons offered for sale are wild–caught babies.

Signs of a Healthy Dragon

It may be difficult to assess a water dragon's health by just looking in its enclosure, so ask to hold the lizard for closer inspection. Familiarize yourself with the appearance of a healthy water dragon of proper body weight and settle for no less.

This list will help you find a healthy dragon.

- Make sure the water dragon has acceptable body weight.
- Check to make sure there are no external blemishes such as bite marks, skin tears, sores, rashes, etc.
- The eyes should be clear and not sunken into the head. They should be open and not half closed
- Check the nostrils, and vent to make sure they are clean and free of obstructions.
- Look closely for the presence of mites on the skin, especially in tight places like the armpits.
- Check for kinks in the spine, pelvis, and tail bones.
- Watch the dragon climbing in the enclosure. If it has difficulty climbing or moving around, this may indicate the dragon has a serious problem.

region inexpensively. But this might not always be the case. In the past, we have often seen countries decide to prohibit the export of wildlife (countries like Australia, South Africa, and more recently, Thailand). If that were to happen, supplies would dry up within weeks.

The mass importation of these animals and, consequently, their low price discourages commercial breeding attempts. Breeding them will cost more than the price of importing wild-caught babies. As a result, buyers should be skeptical of claims that green water dragons offered for sale are captive bred. It is all too easy to buy imported green water dragon babies and sell them as captive bred, because it is not possible to know the difference, and because the price for captive bred ones is much higher. The honest breeder must possess at least enough breeder animals to make purchase of additional imported animals unnecessary and have the appropriate caging for doing so.

When purchasing green water dragons, keep in mind the fact that you will almost always be buying animals that are taken from the wild. Also, being of a relatively low value

Captive Bred vs. Wild Caught

The terms captive bred and wild caught are frequently used by reptile hobbyists. A captive-bred animal was hatched (or born) in captivity, usually from parents who mated and laid their eggs (or gave birth) in captivity. In contrast, wild-caught animals were taken from the wild and sent to wholesalers, importers, or other animal dealers.

Captive-bred reptiles and amphibians are usually preferred over wild-caught ones. Wild-caught animals usually are carrying parasites and possibly have other illnesses and injuries that the new owner will have to remedy. Additionally, some wild-caught animals fail to adapt to captivity, withering away and dying in a few weeks or months. Hobbyists who are concerned with depleting wild populations of animals usually avoid wild-caught animals.

Captive-bred animals usually do not have these problems. However, the hobbyist should be aware that it is possible for captive-bred animals to acquire parasites and other illnesses if they come into contact with infected individuals. Buying a captive-bred water dragon does not guarantee that your pet will be healthy, but it does increase the chance that it will be.

for importers and dealers, green water dragon babies are often mistreated during importation and housing before sale. Consequently, many have suffered a lot before arriving at the pet shop.

In the wild, these baby lizards always avoid each other and spread out, but in captivity they are forced into cages without being given adequate space in an effort to keep costs down. Animals that look skinny, have their eyes closed, and/or have remnants of feces sticking to their tail roots will most likely not live for many more weeks or even days. Also avoid purchasing "tame" animals, ones that "can be handled." Those animals referred to as tame are often the sick ones within the group, too sick to worry about an approaching hand. If you have a choice, take the babies that are shy, and hard to catch. A missing finger or tip of a tail is less important than purchasing an alert, healthy animal that reacts to your approaching hand by running away.

Another thing to consider when purchasing animals in a pet shop is avoiding those in which you routinely see a variety of lizards kept in the same terrarium. Lizards from various parts of the world often carry different parasites. Some of these parasites will not have any ill effects on lizards that live in a common environment, but the same parasites may be lethal to those from other parts of the world. Look for clean water bowls and overall clean conditions inside the terrarium, as that will reduce the odds that the lizards you purchase carry pathogens.

In both species of water dragon it is very hard to find adults and subadults for sale. These can most often be found on occasion when a private owner wants to sell his or her pet. Keeping this in mind, if you think you will want to breed water dragons you need to purchase enough babies at the start. If you want to end up with a pair, odds are very slim that this is possible by buying just two or three unsexed babies. Quite often, by the time they are adults, one or two lizards may have died or escaped. Australian water dragons have a high survival rate, but it is still quite possible that several years after purchase you may be left with only two adult animals of the same sex. At that point, you might put in a request to purchase an adult of the opposite sex, and as they tend to sell out quickly, you may not find any for sale. Start with at least four or five babies. Selling surplus males as single animals is not hard because they are usually the more desirable ones. Having too many females is not a problem either because one male can be kept with several females.

Playing the Odds

If you are considering breeding water dragons, buying only two or three unsexed babies may not be sufficient. It's best to purchase at least five or six animals so the odds are quite good that you will end up with at least a breeding pair or two after a few years.

Because Australia does not export wildlife, virtually all Australian water dragons in the pet trade are captive-bred.

Bringing Your New Water Dragon Home
Acclimation

It is important to accommodate newly purchased water dragons correctly. At first, it is necessary to consider that the water dragons will be stressed due to changing environments and transport. For this reason, you need to give them as much rest as possible during the first few weeks. You can do this by covering most of the transparent (glass) sides of the terrarium. That way, any movement that takes place outside of the enclosure will not disturb them. Also, they will better learn the limits of their space; if they were to run into the glass, they would only become confused and more stressed and may even hurt their noses. To make your water dragons feel safer, you also need to give them ample hiding places.

Lighting and Temperature

The proper amount of light and comfortable temperatures inside the terrarium are key factors in your newly purchased water dragon's comfort. Although an ultraviolet B (UVB) light is needed, it is not urgent for the first few days. UVB is used by the lizards to make vitamin D, which in turn helps the animals absorb calcium from their food. Initially, they may not be eating much, so it's not as important to have the light until later on.

It is important to keep water dragons at the correct temperature, which should not be too high. Many people place young babies in a terrarium that is too warm, which may kill them within days or weeks. In nature, water dragons will experience ambient air temperatures in the 70s (about 21°-26°C), or more often in the 80s (about 27°-31°C). Therefore, it is best to keep them in the mid– to high 70s (about 23°-26°C), with a warmer spot on one end of the terrarium. Temperatures in the 90s (about 32°-37°C) or more will

Water dragons are often nervous lizards. Give your new pet time to acclimate to its new surroundings.

Quarantine any newly acquired reptile in a properly outfitted enclosure.

stress the animals and may even be lethal to them. Many young green water dragons will have parasites, and very high temperatures will drastically increase metabolism, which could be fatal to infected or diseased organs.

It is best to have a temperature gradient in the terrarium (temperatures ranging from a lower to higher one) to see which end the newly purchased water dragon prefers to stay in. If he is always at the cold end, the overall temperature may be too high, while if he is always at the warmest end, the temperature may be too low. Humidity levels are also important. At the lowest temperature, relative air humidity is higher, and therefore a lizard that spends most of the time at the cool end of the terrarium may also want to choose that end because of the higher humidity there. If you increase the humidity to check for this and he still stays at the cool end, you can be sure that the lizard is there only because he prefers the lower temperature.

Quarantine

You should always put your recently purchased animals in quarantine, especially if the new lizard will be housed with others eventually. The word quarantine is derived from Latin

Winter Fasting

If you purchase Australian water dragons in winter, they may not eat for the first days or even weeks because they are hibernating. In that case, you can have them continue hibernation for a while, or keep them in a warm terrarium until they start eating on their own, whichever is more suitable to you.

and means that the people for which it is intended need to be separated from others for 40 days. Sometimes, 40 days may not be sufficient, but you can never be sure. Occasionally, people can live healthy lives while carrying parasites that are dangerous to others. Therefore, to be safe, it is obvious that the longer the quarantine period is, the better. There are two common mistakes people make. The first is not quarantining their animals. The second is to make the quarantine terrarium a stress-provoking prison for their new lizards. The enclosure you use for quarantine should be appropriate and provide the already stressed newcomers with a good home and excellent living conditions.

Quarantine the new dragon in an appropriately outfitted terrarium, but observe it closely for signs of health issues. You should probably use a newspaper or paper towel substrate, so that you can monitor the appearance of the feces. If the feces are bloody, runny, or worm-ridden, you should seek the consultation of a reptile veterinarian. Also consult a vet if any other health issues manifest during quarantine. It is best if the quarantine terrarium is as far as possible from any other reptiles you may have.

Feeding Your New Arrival

Newly purchased water dragons may not want to eat at first, or better said, may not appear to eat. When insects are offered to them in a feeding dish, they simply may not be recognized as food in this new environment. If that's the case, try placing a few moving insects or earthworms loose inside the terrarium. Usually, the water dragons will be attracted to the moving insects and begin eating them.

If they still do not eat the insects, you must try something else. Cover the sides of the terrarium with paper, an old curtain, or something else, and open a peephole so you can check the lizards. Then, throw in small moving worms or insects and watch them. In order to survive in nature, an animal needs to eat, but *must not be eaten*. Sometimes the fear instinct is stronger than the appetite—especially in baby lizards! In nature, baby lizards are much more vulnerable because of their smaller size. So, when you feed them, you'll notice that they may freeze in order not to be seen by predators and be eaten; while frozen they will

Still Not Eating!

So, if you followed all of these instructions and one of your newly purchased lizards is still not eating, you may have a lizard that does not want to eat because it's sick. Do not force-feed it! When a lizard does not want to eat, it instinctually knows that it cannot digest the food because of its illness. If you force-feed such a lizard, you would in most cases only speed up his decline and death. But you can go halfway—you can insert some yogurt or sour cream into a small syringe and put a small drop of it on the tip of the lizard's snout without blocking the airflow through its nostrils. You can also put a drop on its lips. Lizards will usually lick it and get some nutrition. The acid of that sour cream or yogurt may stimulate the function of the stomach, as well. Don't feed too much in one session. Feed just a drop and then another small drop several hours later. After that, your lizard may start eating moving insects.

ignore the moving insects as well. Don't worry; as they grow and learn that you do not present any danger to them, this shyness will diminish (if you are wise enough not to put your chasing hand inside the terrarium every day to grab them, which will keep them fearful longer.) People often write to me about their young water dragons not eating. Well, they may never have seen them eat, and yet they did not become skinny. These water dragons would only start chasing the insects after people left them alone in their habitats.

Unlike this tame dragons, most newly purchased ones will be too nervous to eat while being watched.

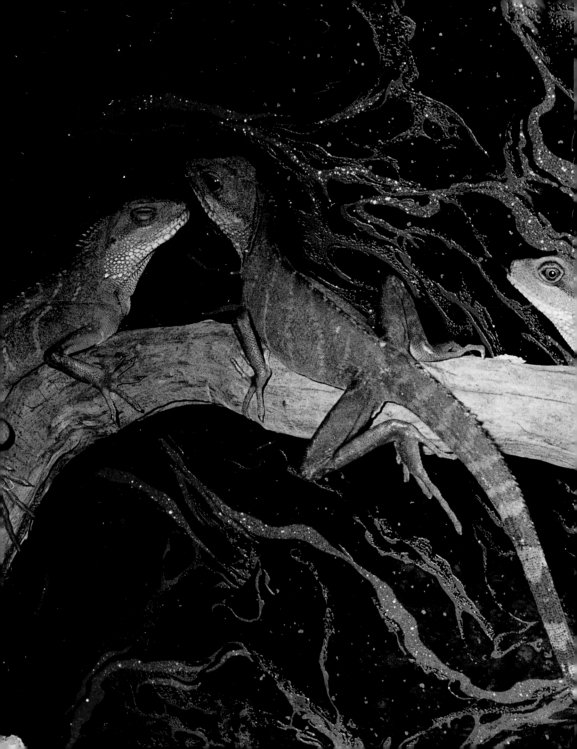

Chapter 2

Housing

Creating the proper habitat is critical to the long-term health of your water dragon. Water dragons are adapted to live in warm humid areas, so they won't be able to survive in the average living room or suburban backyard. You will have to create a habitat for your pet that provides the temperature, humidity, lighting, and other conditions that will make him healthy and comfortable.

Green water dragons dwell in humid tropical forests and need to be housed accordingly.

Indoor Terraria

For both species of water dragon, similar types of terraria can be used. In order to build or purchase the appropriate terrarium, you need to have several things in mind. First, due to the size of the animals, you need to consider fairly large enclosures. For an adult pair of water dragons, the terrarium must be at least 4 x 4 feet wide and 5 feet high (1.2 m x 1.2 m wide and 1.5 m high) or larger. Second, the animals like to climb and will need branches that are about as wide as their bodies. Therefore, it is good to have adequate vertical space. Next, the water dragons need a water basin to bathe in. As they typically defecate in water, the basin needs to be placed in such a way that daily cleaning becomes an easy task.

Last, if for some reason they panic, water dragons may bounce their noses against the glass sides of the terrarium, which can cause injury. This is, therefore, why you need more vertical than horizontal space—if you have less horizontal space, the animals cannot reach very much speed while running. Having transparent glass on all sides should be avoided. It is much better to cover or paint three of the sides.

Materials

When planning construction of your terrarium, it is best to only use glass for the front panel. It is even better to make the lowest 10 inches (25.4 cm) or so opaque; you can make this portion a ventilation screen. There should also be a ventilation screen at the top of the terrarium, so that air can flow from the bottom to the top. The warmer air inside a heated indoor enclosure will flow upward and help to keep it well ventilated. Having a top screen also makes it possible for you to place any spotlights and UVB lights (more on this topic later) just outside and above the terrarium. Use aluminum screens because plastic screens may melt from the heat. Also, if the lizards can reach these lights, they may burn themselves or get electrocuted. Quite often, accidents happen when heat lamps are placed inside enclosures. You need to make sure that there are no other flammable objects near heat sources as well.

The sides and back of the terrarium are best made of opaque materials like wood, metal, fiberglass, or plastic. Because the air inside the terrarium needs to be kept humid, choose materials on which fungi cannot grow. For placement of a door, you can use the front panel or one of the side panels; choose whatever option is easier in your situation. When you have more than one water dragon in a terrarium, it is better to consider using two small doors at either side of the terrarium so that all areas can be reached. Also, keep in mind that water dragons will not slip out as easily if these doors are kept small. It is not good to be chasing your lizard from room to room before finally capturing him because he will be stand-offish for the weeks or months to come after such an adventure.

Metal Screens Only

For any screening needed for the terrarium, it's best to use metal. Fiberglass or plastic screening should be avoided because escaped feeder insects may chew through it and make an opening through which the lizards can escape. Also, mice may want to get inside the terrarium to get to the feeder dish and could chew a hole in soft screening.

Water

The water basin does not need to be very large. Over the years I have kept and bred hundreds of water dragons and have concluded that a water bowl that the animal can just fit into is large enough. The problem with larger water basins is cleaning them. Even if you used a larger water basin and let it empty through a tap at the bottom of the terrarium, you'd still need to consider having no more than a bucketful of water in it so that daily cleaning could be kept as easy as possible. Since water dragons defecate in water, cleaning is necessary on a daily basis or at least every other day.

Temperature

It is important to create conditions in the terrarium that resemble the water dragon's natural habitat. It is easiest and most natural to use heat lamps to maintain the proper temperature, since water dragons heat themselves in nature by basking in the sunlight.

If your terrarium gets too cool at night, you can use red light bulbs. The light produced by these bulbs will not disturb the day-night cycle of your lizards. Another option is to use a ceramic heat emitter. This device produces a lot of heat but no light, making it ideal for nighttime heating of a terrarium. Because it produces so much heat, a ceramic heat emitter needs to be housed in a ceramic socket. All of these items are available at well-stocked pet stores, hardware stores, and online retailers.

When setting up lighting, fix the heat lamps and the UVB light (see UVB light section) close together so that the water dragons will receive UVB while basking. When you have these items on top of the terrarium above the aluminum screen, you will create a warmer area at the top of the terrarium and a cooler half at the bottom; this way the animals can better thermo-regulate, or in other words, they can

Water dragons control their body temperature by moving into and out of patches of sunlight.

regulate their body temperature by moving to a warmer or cooler place as they feel the need. It is very important to give the animals a choice and to have an environment with a sufficient temperature gradient, which means it offers a difference in temperature within that limited space.

Water dragons do not require too much heat. Many people keep them too warm, and as a result, some may do poorly or even die. The mid- to upper 70s (about 23°-26°C) is fine as an average terrarium temperature, and during the day the hotter top section of the terrarium may be in the lower to mid-90s (about 33°-35°C).

You can check the preferences of the water dragons by seeing where they prefer to be. If they are always at the cool end, they either want to get away from too much heat, or they are trying to find a place with higher air humidity. The cooler side of a space is almost always the side with higher air humidity. At night the temperature can be lower.

UVB Light

The use of UVB light is a complex issue. One of the problems is that you cannot see it. Another is that the terrarium keeper needs to have some understanding of physics in order to understand its proper use.

Light is split up into wavelengths, some of which are the ultraviolet B waves. Only a small portion of UVB light is really working to form much needed vitamin D3 in the skin. This small portion is around 300 nm (a nanometer (nm) is a wavelength; it stands for one billionth of a meter). Therefore, you will need to buy a light that emits UVB around 300 nm. Most UV lights made for plants will not work. You need to purchase a special UVB light made for lizards to be at least in the neighborhood of proper light for them. The term

When housing water dragons indoors, you must provide an artificial source of ultraviolet B light.

"neighborhood" is used because lizards from various climates have very different needs. Lizards like Chinese crocodile lizards (*Shinisaurus*) and monkey–tailed skinks (*Corucia*) will need less UVB light than lizards like the *Uromastyx* species, for instance. It is impossible to find out the real optimal needs for UVB light in all of the different species of reptiles, so you need to understand that we are in a trial and error situation when it comes to gauging the appropriate amount.

Another problem is that condensation forms on the inside of these lights over time, especially in the case of fluorescent tubes. As a result, UVB light will be gradually blocked over time and will eventually diminish. As a rule of thumb, you need to replace these lights every year; while more frequent replacement is better, it can be rather costly. There are also incandescent bulbs that generate UVB and are marketed for use by reptile keepers. They generate heat, visible light, and UVB, and many keepers consider them to be the best bulbs available. Although they are much more costly than fluorescent bulbs, they need to be replaced only every three to five years, making them more economical in the long run.

If you could install a spectrometer—a device that measures the wavelengths of light—you would be able to read how much UVB is emitted. With the same spectrometer you can also check the amount of UVB light emitted from the morning sun so you could have an idea of how close you are to appropriate emission from natural light as well. But lizards do not need to be in the sun all day in order to get enough UVB light.

Keeping this in mind, you can do without UVB lights and their various problems by putting your terrarium near a window on the east or west side of your house; one or two hours of *direct* sunlight will do the job. Direct or unfiltered sunlight must enter the terrarium by screen; normal window glass filters away nearly all UVB light, as does terrarium glass. Only use this method if the majority of the enclosure is made of screen. If the enclosure is mostly glass, fatal overheating can result. Remember this when using UVB generating bulbs; if there is glass between the bulb and the lizard, the UVB will be filtered out.

If you decide to use UVB light, you will need to consider the distance from the UVB light source to the basking lizard, which is a very important factor. The energy of the UVB waves will spread over a larger surface area when they are farther away from the source. For example, when a lizard is 2 feet (61 cm) away from the light source instead of 1 foot (30.5 cm), the energy is spread over a surface that is four times greater, which means that at 2 feet (61 cm) the lizard will receive four times less UVB light than at a 1-foot (30.5 cm) distance. But at 3 feet (91.4 cm), the amount is already 9 times less. Therefore, you need to get the lizards close to the UVB light source by placing the basking spot near the light.

Outdoors, with natural sunlight, the distance from the sun does not matter at all, but with artificially generated UVB light you need to always watch that your lizards get the proper amount. It may also occur that one lizard in a group is always chased away from the basking area and will spend more time on the floor of the terrarium. Under these conditions, such a lizard will not receive enough UVB light.

In winter, when Australian water dragons

Do Some Homework

You will gain a lot of insight into your dragon's behavior and natural history if you learn about the natural conditions in the water dragon's habitat and try to imitate them. Nowadays, you can go online to find climates for almost any town in the world for more exact information on the proper environment for your lizards.

Live plants and a sphagnum moss substrate will help maintain the high humidity your dragon needs.

hibernate and do not eat much or at all, UVB light is not as necessary because not much calcium needs to be digested. On the other hand, when you feed your young water dragons a lot in order to make them grow faster, they will need more calcium so their bones and muscles will grow just as fast as the rest of their bodies, which means they will need more UVB light. Fast-growing lizards that do not receive enough UVB light will have problems like weak bones that break easily, short jaw bones, or trembling as a result of cramps in their calcium-deficient muscles.

Humidity

Maintaining good humidity levels in a terrarium is the toughest thing to do, especially in winter when the temperature in the enclosure will be higher than room temperature, and also when the room itself is much drier than in summer. At higher temperatures, evaporation will be greater and humidity will escape. Therefore, in order to maintain good humidity levels in an indoor terrarium, you need to use to some sort of misting system. You do not need to use that system all day long; the best time to use it is around early morning because, as in nature, the relative air humidity is higher then. As mentioned, heating will make humidity escape.

You can hand–mist your dragons with a plant mister. These are bottles with a spray nozzle available at home improvement stores and plant nurseries. There are several styles; the ones that can be left in the "on" position are the most useful, because you don't have to keep squeezing a trigger. Another option is to use one of the commercially available misting systems. You can get these from various reptile supply companies online or at herp shows. These are great when you have a number of enclosures to spray, but are often too much for one enclosure. When using a commercial misting system, you have a place for all the water to go. Most hobbyists position the enclosure over a tray or tub that the water drips down into.

The ideal humidity for water dragons is 65 to 70 percent. Drops down to 50 percent can be tolerated for a little while but should be avoided if possible. Using a hygrometer (a device that measures humidity) is strongly recommended. Some pet stores—especially those that have alarge reptile section—carry hygrometers.

Avoid excessive misting. In nature, water dragons will bask and dry their bodies during the day and need to do this regularly. If you keep them at humidity levels that are too high all the time, blisters may result. They may initially appear on the belly, where you may not notice them before they worsen, a situation you want o avoid.

Hiding Areas

Water dragons will feel much safer and more comfortable if they have several hiding places. You can use hollow tree trunks or cork bark tubes or simply make small boxes for them to hide in. This will also help prevent them from panicking and bouncing their noses against the glass walls of their terraria.

Be Careful of the Sun

If you are using a glass enclosure, be careful when you position it. You do not want the terrarium to be in direct sunlight for any significant part of the day. Glass holds heat fairly well, so with sunlight streaming in, the temperature inside the terrarium will rise dramatically, possibly killing your water dragon.

With the addition of a water bowl and some climbing branches, this enclosure will be perfect for a young water dragon.

Plants

Plants are also important in the terrarium. Pineapples are usually a good choice in a large terrarium. These plants are very strong, and water dragons can walk over them without damaging them. Also, they can live with very little available soil, which is often the case inside these terraria. They are easy to purchase. You can buy a pineapple, twist off (don't cut) the top, let it dry a few days, and then lay it on top of garden soil at warm temperatures. Within weeks, roots will emerge and the plant will grow.

A second type of plant for these lizards is *Ficus benjamini*. A small problem with *Ficus benjamini* is that its branches can grow through fine screen. This may start with a small thin twig that will eventually grow thicker, damaging the screen. All you need to do is cut off any small branches that make their way through the screen. Other plants that do well are *Scindapsis*, *Sansevieria*, *Schefflera* and *Hibiscus*. Avoid any spiny plants like *Bougainvillea*. It is a good

Why Outdoors?

There are a number of reasons why housing water dragons outdoors can be good for them. The primary benefit of outdoor housing is the exposure to natural sunlight, which contributes to calcium metabolism and stimulates natural behaviors. Also, there is the space. Outdoor enclosures can be much larger than most indoor ones. This increased space gives your dragon more exercise and more of an ability to act as it would in the wild.

idea to have several extra plants, so you can switch out any that become ragged from being in the terrarium.

Outdoor Terraria

Depending on the climate in which you live, you may want to consider using an outdoor terrarium. At Agama International, Inc., in central Alabama, I have successfully used outdoor terraria to house and breed Australian water dragons. In this area of the US, they can live outdoors all year in terraria specially designed for that purpose. I have also kept green water dragons in the same terraria for the summer. In southern Florida you can keep both species outdoors in this type of terrarium throughout the year, and in the northern parts of the country you can use them during the summer months for both species.

The author's outdoor terraria in progress. They are built into the ground to provide a more stable temperature.

Construction

When I designed my outdoor terraria I wanted to create an optimal microclimate for the lizards. Outdoors and unprotected by a specially designed habitat, Alabama's climate would be too hot in some summers and too cold in most, if not all, winters. The main consideration I had was to create a microclimate in which these extremes of temperature did not occur. This also needed to be accomplished without external use of electricity. In the first place, it would save money; but also, as I have experienced, an unexpected situation, like a blizzard, can knock out power for days, putting your animals at great risk. In many cases, electricity would be needed most during extremely cold weather.

The best way to create a favorable climate is by sinking these terraria into the ground. The deeper you place them, the more stable the microclimate will be. Also, using concrete or block walls below ground level will provide a more stable microclimate, as they will stay cooler in summer and warmer in winter. You can, of course, build an above-ground terrarium, but the conditions will be less stable.

Below are instructions for building my outdoor terraria. The sizes given assume you are keeping a breeding group of one male and two or three females. If you are keeping fewer water dragons, you can make the terrarium smaller than the dimensions given.

Step 1: Dig a hole that is about 2 feet (0.6m) deep in an east-west direction. The hole should slope slightly from one end to the other for better drainage and be about 10 feet by 10 feet (3.0 m). At the northern side of terrarium, build a higher earth level, which is needed for a more favorable microclimate. Do this by throwing all the dirt on top of the northern side.

Step 2: Build the southern and northern walls with building or cinder blocks. Before building those walls, pour thick concrete on the place where the walls come and fix a half inch rebar inside that concrete. The walls should be all about 8 feet apart (2.4 m), so that later the 8 foot plywood for pouring the square walls would fit nicely. It is handy to incorporate openings for hiding in the northern wall, using clay pipes for example.

An Australian water dragon inside one of the author's outdoor enclosures.

Step 3: Inside the future terrarium, dig a narrow ditch very close to the south wall from one end to the other end. Place a corrugated black plastic drainage tube with holes inside, in such a way that about one third will stick out of the ditch. The ditch and tube will create drainage for the terrarium and help prevent flooding.

Step 4: Build the end wall at the lowest level and build it over the drainage tube that comes out at this end, allowing it exit the wall and terrarium. Block the end of the drainage tube with half–inch sturdy mesh wire to prevent rodents from entering and chewing holes in the tube.

Step 5: Pour the concrete floor inbetween those walls in such a way that about a quarter of the drainage tube will stick out.

Step 6: Use two 4 ft. x 8 ft. (1.2 m x 2.4 m) pieces of sturdy plywood to make forms to put the concrete between. If the plywood is not strong enough we need to make it stronger by screwing a few long pieces of wood on the outside. This way we can do one square wall every second day, as the concrete needs to harden before the plywood can be removed.

Step 7: Use that same plywood to make overhanging pieces of concrete at the northern side of the terraria. These pieces of concrete must rest on the flat parts of the square walls and must contain enough rebars for strength. We can do two terraria at a time, but need to wait three days before removal of the plywood and do the next two.

Step 8: Build the east-west wall, two blocks high over the southern edge of the overhanging pieces of concrete. Then, a few days later, fill up the access dirt on top of the overhanging concrete to this two block high wall.

Step 9: Make a southward slope inside the terraria with topsoil. This will allow the water to drain in the ditch you created earlier. You are now ready to add plants, water bowls, and hiding places.

Step 10: Cover the top with a strong wire mesh—half-inch (1.3 cm) is recommended—and build in a door. After that, you can make the top out of strong half inch wire and also make an entrance door for every terrarium.

In winter the terraria are covered with transparent plastic sheets, which rest on the tilted wire so that rainwater will move to the southern side of the terraria. The plastic will filter out UVB light from the sun; but, luckily, in winter this light is not needed as the animals do not eat then and thus have nothing to digest.

Recommended Plants

There is a wide variety of plants you can use to landscape your outdoor terrarium. A short list is below. Be aware that not all plants will thrive in every climate, so be sure to find out if the varieties you like will survive in your locale.

Ficus

Forsythia

Grape

Hibiscus

Lantana camara

Mulberry

Pineapple

Sansevieria

Inside the Terrarium

Plants In outdoor terraria, you can use some of the same plants as in the indoor terrarium. Pineapples work in either setup. These plants tolerate dry and wet weather and temperatures down to the freezing point. Another excellent choice is the *Lantana camara*, also called *Verbena*, a bush that grows up to 6 feet (1.8 m) high and has nice yellow and red flowers. You may want to choose this plant as Hoser (1989) mentions habitats overgrown with *Lantanas* are preferred by water dragons. Other plants are *Hibiscus* (which are not very cold hearty), *Ficus benjamini*, or *Sansevierea*.

Breeding For rearing young babies that will eventually be moved into larger enclosures, you can build terraria out of corrugated sheets of galvanized steel. This steel is often used for roofing or for building warehouses. It goes about 2 feet (61 cm) into the ground so that moles, shrews, etc., will stay out. It is 2.5 feet (76.2 cm) high above the ground and smooth on both sides so that the lizards cannot escape and snakes or mice cannot get in. These terraria can be about 100 sq feet (30.5 sq m) and hold up to 200 baby water dragons.

There is a higher ridge in the middle, so that the screen over it has two slopes. For screening, you can use wire mesh fencing with 2 x 4 inch (5.1 x 10.2 m) openings. This is very strong and made for outdoor use. It only needs to keep bigger birds, cats, opossums, and raccoons out, because the lizards cannot reach the wire anyway. The extra benefit is that when feeding you do not need to open a door because you can throw feeder insects in through the wire. Also, in the fall, when night frosts begin, you can lay plastic over the roof and it won't fill with rainwater, which would happen over a horizontal screen. You will also need to make a door.

Inside the enclosure, lizards will live directly on the earth. You should have pipes or tubes running underground that can be used as hiding places when weather is cold or hot. You will also need to provide several branches of wood on which the lizards can perch. For this,

Climbing branches are essential furniture for a water dragon terrarium.

you can use old cardboard boxes because they will also provide many small areas where the animals are able to hide from each other if they want to do so.

Outdoor terraria that lack ground contact and are placed on top of a table or concrete floor are dangerous to use in warmer climates because these terraria can get overheated easily and kill the lizards inside. Unfortunately, this happens all too often when people attempt to keep lizards outdoors without researching proper housing conditions for their animals.

Water Bowl or Pond For water dragons, place the pond or water bowl in a central location in the terrarium. If you choose a plastic bowl, be aware that lizards may not be able to get out of the water because of the smooth sides of such a bowl. Try to find a container with a sloping side, like a paint roller pan. Otherwise, you will have to put pieces of wood, like branches, or other floating objects at the edges of the bowl so that the water dragons will not drown hopelessly swimming about trying to find a way out. On occasion, a branch that stands tilted at the edge of the bowl can fall into the water, so that it ceases to function as a ladder for the lizards to climb out on. Therefore, be sure that all branches are well secured, or that their length extends beyond the rim of the container. Also, a floating piece of wood may eventually sink after it has absorbed too much water.

Small water bowls need to be cleaned daily, with the exception of those for Australian water dragons during the winter season. A larger bowl in an indoor terrarium can be cleaned by having a drain and tap at its shallow end, or you can install a pump and filtering system. Water dragons will defecate in the water, and the more they eat, the faster the water will get dirty. Therefore, the bowl should be located in a place it can be easily reached; otherwise, you may start neglecting cleaning chores.

After washing, refill the bowl with water that is a comfortable temperature—water dragons will not check the temperature before jumping in. Except for Australian water dragons, during winter the temperature of the water should be between 65° and 85°F (about 18° and 29°F). If the water bowl is in an outdoor terrarium, try to place it in shade or partial shade. Small bowls can get overheated when placed in the sun during summer.

Water dragons kept outdoors often have more intense colors than those kept indoors.

When water is too cold, it most likely will not kill the animal directly, but may cause cramping or weakening of the muscles, which may result in their drowning, especially if the water is too deep or if the sides of the bowl are too smooth for them to get out. Therefore, it is always safer to fill water bowls only 3-4 inches (7.4-10.2 cm) in winter, especially in the case of hibernating Australian water dragons. If you keep Australian water dragons outdoors in a large pond, be sure to provide lots of branches and other means for them to get out of the water easily.

Glass Houses

You can use a small greenhouse as your water dragon enclosure. If you are careful in how you outfit the greenhouse, the lizards can be allowed to roam without any other containment. One thing you must remember is your dragons' need to thermoregulate. There must be the appropriate range of temperatures throughout the greenhouse. Another point to remember is that the glass will screen out the vital ultraviolet light. Supplemental UV lights will be necessary. Lastly, you have to make sure the greenhouse is escape-proof. Having two doors at each entry will help with containing the lizards, as they will have to get through two doors to escape.

For larger outdoor ponds, you can rely on the natural cleansing process of water. To facilitate this, you can use animals like tubifex or plants like water hyacinths or lotus. However, over time the water will become richer in food and nutrients, so be sure to pull out water hyacinths, which tend to overgrow easily, to remove surplus food from the water. You can also guide water from roofs and gutters into pipes leading to the bottom of these ponds. That way, the pond water is being cleansed every time it rains.

Greenhouses

If you plan to keep terraria that have no ground contact inside of a greenhouse, you are entering a danger zone. There are numerous stories about lizards dying because of overheating. Imagine that you a have a large aquarium-style terrarium on a table in a greenhouse. Typically, the sun will warm it up, and the terrarium will get additional heat as well. But then that unusually warm spring day arrives and you are not at home to check on the animals. On a day like this, the heat inside the terrarium can build up and may reach beyond 100°F (about 37.8°C) by afternoon. Because the lizards have nowhere to go to get away from the heat, you may come home to find your lizards have died. If you are putting your terrarium inside a greenhouse, it is best to use a screen enclosure.

If you are planning to house your terraria inside a greenhouse, you must make them in such a way that they all have sufficient ground contact. With ground contact, thermal energy is easily exchanged with the earth by means of conduction. The terraria can either be built inside the back wall of the greenhouse with ceramic tubes inserted inside the

The primary benefit of outdoor housing is exposing your dragon to natural sunlight.

wall, or on the floor with tubes inserted into the ground. The tubes will serve as cool retreats for the lizards if they get too hot.

For terraria that will be placed on a table, you will have to use objects that take a long time to get hot or, in other words, objects that can store a lot of thermal energy, inside the terrarium. Such an object could theoretically be a very large stone, but that may be too impractical due to the weight of the stone needed. An easier alternative is to use water. By weight, water can store much more thermal energy; however, by volume, there is not much difference between the use of water, sand, stones, or a block that is filled with sand or concrete. Water has an additional advantage in that it can evaporate, which takes a lot of thermal energy. You need to refill any evaporated water regularly, though.

Next, place a plastic shoebox or sweater box inside the terrarium. This box can be put on top of two laths of wood so that a small hiding space will be created beneath it. Lizards prefer to escape to a cozy space they just fit into because it feels safe. Then, fill the box with water. Before you put the lid on the box, punch one or two round openings in it. Then cut one or two pieces of aluminum screen that are just a bit larger than the openings. With a hot soldering gun, simply affix the screen to the lid over the openings. Let the hot gun stay on the screen until it sinks into the plastic and let it sit until the plastic hardens. Do this on several points around each opening. By using a lid with screened openings, you are able to add fresh water, and at the same time, prevent the lizards from falling into the cooling water supply. Also, the opening allows water to evaporate when conditions get warm, which takes away a lot of thermal energy. This is, in fact, air conditioning in its most primitive form.

The amount of water needed depends entirely on the conditions in the environment. Of course, in hotter climates you will have to put more water in a larger box. However, before using this system, it's a good idea to test it for several weeks during summer by putting a maximum-minimum thermometer under the box. These boxes will also provide safer places for the lizards in the event of very cold weather.

Also, remember that because glass will filter out UVB, steps should be taken to give lizards kept inside glass-covered greenhouses their necessary portion of UVB light. As mentioned earlier, you can do this by removing glass and replacing it with screening or by using UVB lights. There is also a certain type of Plexiglas on the market that should let enough UVB light through, but it can be expensive. Before purchasing, be sure to check that 300 nanometer wavelengths will not be absorbed by it.

Although water dragons are from warm climates, they can overheat. Your enclosure must provide a range of temperatures.

Chapter 3

Feeding and Nutrition

Both species of water dragon are omnivorous. They eat a variety of insects, worms, fish, and other small vertebrates. However, plant material has also been found in the stomachs and feces of both species. It seems that they eat more vegetarian food in nature than they do in captive conditions. The reason for this is not yet fully understood. Quite possibly, they may prefer the insects, worms, and small vertebrates, but cannot catch enough to eat and, therefore, have to consume plant matter in order to get enough food.

You see similar behavior with other types of lizards in terraria. Tegus, for instance, also tend to eat less plant material in captivity than in nature. Research was done on the stomach contents of Argentine tegus in the wild, and it was found that about 70 percent of their diet was plant matter, while in captivity they would mainly eat animal matter (Mercolli and Yanusky, 1994). Most vegetarian species, like iguanas and *Uromastyx*, also consume more insects and other animal food in captivity than they would be able to catch in their natural habitats. This could, however, be a direct consequence of being offered too many insects and other animals in the terrarium environment.

Feeding your lizards too much animal matter can cause some problems, however. When not well gut-loaded, insects will lack many necessary nutrients, like calcium and carotenes for example. At a minimum, it is important to feed your water dragons a lot of plants, especially leaves, so they will get some of the necessary nutritional ingredients that are found in plants and usually lacking in insects (see the chapter on health).

You can try to make your lizards eat plant material by not giving them access to insects or small vertebrates on certain days. Similarly, I have seen this pattern with my Argentine tegus, *Tupinambis merianae*. If I fed them

A female Australian water dragon eyeing the prey in her feeding dish.

mice, rats, and cantaloupes simultaneously, they would gorge themselves on the rodents and not touch the cantaloupes. However, if I fed them only cantaloupes, they would accept them as food. A lack of vegetable matter in the diet will also make the food content higher in proteins, and too much protein can cause kidney problems. Water dragons that refuse plant foods obtain vegtable matter from the gut contents of feeder insects.

Insect Foods
Black Soldier Flies

When you are able to keep water dragons in outdoor habitats, you will have less difficulty feeding them, especially the babies. Outdoors, you can put bait in the terraria to attract flies, you can feed termites with little worry, and you can breed fruit flies. One of the preferred foods for young water dragons is the black soldier fly, *Hermetia illuscens*. These flies are native to a large part of the US. They prefer warmer climates and are spreading throughout the world rapidly as they are moved with potted plants, etc. In Queensland, Australia, they are called American soldier flies. They are very prolific—a few flies landing on your compost hill will result in thousands of larvae a couple of weeks later.

Catch Your Bugs

Some hobbyists like to collect insects and other invertebrates to feed their lizards. There is nothing wrong with this practice, and your lizards will benefit from the variety. However there are some risks. Wild-collected insects may harbor parasites. You must also be sure that you are collecting from areas that are not sprayed with pesticides, fungicides, or fertilizers. Many city parks spray for mosquitoes, so check with your municipality before you collect from the local park. Finally there are some types of invertebrates that are dangerous to feed to your pets. The species listed below are toxic, vicious, or otherwise dangerous to feed to your pet.

- **Ants**
- **Bees, wasps, hornets**
- **Caterpillars (depending on species)**
- **Centipedes**
- **Fireflies**
- **Lubber grasshoppers**
- **Scorpions**

Your compost hill can contain old wood shavings and manure. Old and overripe fruits and vegetables can also be thrown on top.

Usually, during the second half of April, these soldier flies emerge from their pupa and start breeding. By July, after the first lizard babies are hatched, there is an endless supply of fly larvae in the compost pile. Using a shovel, these larvae can be thrown into the

Wild-collected insects make a good supplement to your water dragon's diet.

terrariums. Many larvae that are not eaten will pupate there and emerge as flies, which are then eaten by the lizards. Others will fly back to the compost hill and lay more eggs, creating the next cycle of larvae. This continues until the fall arrives. Then the remaining larvae will dig deeper into the ground for hibernation and emerge again in April, when the same cycle repeats itself.

Earthworms and Night Crawlers

Earthworms and night crawlers can be bred in a compost pile as well. Old cardboard boxes are flattened, stacked, and placed at the edges of the compost pile. Then, a heavy stone is laid on top. Often, these stacks are partially dug into the compost so that they stay moist. At other edges, old hay is also stacked. In order to enrich the worms with calcium, a few bags of lime are spread over the hay and the cardboard. Lime is a cheap form of calcium. Earthworms will not do well in soil that is too acidic. They prefer a pH value between 5.5 and 6.5 roughly. In general, earthworms appear to be richer in calcium than insects, which has been researched by Zwart in the Netherlands. (Zwart, 1977, 1980).

Table 1 Ca:P Ratio for Various Insects As Compared to Earthworms.

Prey Species	Ca: P (Calcium: Phosphorus)
Crickets (*Gryllus*)	1:3
Locusts	1:7.5
Mealworms	1:3-14
Fly larvae	1:3-10
Earthworms	1:1.4

From the table, you see that earthworms are relatively richer in calcium, compared with the less needed phosphorus, than the insects presented here.

Crickets

House crickets, also referred to as gray crickets, *Acheta domestica*, are the most commonly used feeder insect in the US and Europe. Most pets stores sell crickets—usually in a range of sizes—and larger quantities and specific sizes of crickets are available by special order or through online vendors. When fed a highly nutritious diet—called gut-loading—crickets make a good staple food for your water dragons.

Crickets are mostly fed with foods that are based on grains, like bran and chicken meal. Feed them a lot of green leaves, such as collard greens, dandelions, kale, and mustard greens, as well. In nature, crickets will not have access to these grain products and will eat mostly green leaves. Your water dragons, therefore, need insects fed in the same way. If they are not fed enough green leaves or carrots, they will become more susceptible to parasites (see the chapter health). Because crickets of the genus *Gryllus* will accept green leaves more readily, I prefer to work with them. Most people choose house crickets because they are easier to breed and because most cricket farms sell only this type. Either type of cricket makes a fine food for water dragons.

Breeding Crickets If you keep your water dragons indoors, you are more limited in your choice of food than if they are housed outdoors. When you have only a few animals, it's often easy to buy the food. But if you have many lizards and the food you buy is less reliable, you can consider breeding your own food. Extreme weather conditions in your area in summer or winter may cause an interruption of the supply as well, because during extreme heat or cold it is hard to ship live insects, and next day shipments would make them quite costly. Therefore, in the event that you live in an area where the climate has extremes of weather, you have an extra good reason to breed your own feeder insects.

House crickets must be bred in different containers, because they are kept by age group. These containers must be escape-proof, which is not an easy task when dealing with baby crickets. You can use a strip of Teflon, which can be

Termites make an excellent food for hatchling water dragons but probably should not be fed to lizards housed indoors.

bought as a liquid, around the rim of the container. It makes a very smooth surface over which small crickets cannot walk. Otherwise, you can make a barrier by using wide transparent tape, but it is not easy to stick this tape on the inside corners of the cricket box. A screen top on the container will also work, but you will have some escapes this way.

Crickets can be kept on egg cartons. A problem with this method is that crickets do not thrive, or may even die, when too many fungi start growing on the surface of the cartons. Fungi grow under warm, humid conditions and do even better in the standing air of a poorly ventilated room. Therefore, hot, moist climates can cause problems. I always breed my crickets in a screened barn in the summer, and in winter I keep them in large aluminum containers inside my insect barn. In order to prevent fungi growth, I lower the air humidity inside the cricket boxes by putting heat tape under them when it's cold. The relatively warmer air will result in lower air humidity.

Crickets breed well at temperatures in the upper 70s and lower 80s (about 25°-34°C). The use of a light as a heating element in a cricket box is discouraged because of the risk of starting a fire.

For egg laying, I use flat plastic cups like the containers you use to store food in the refrigerator. Inside these cups, I put a layer of about two inches of loose, moist garden soil. I let the adult crickets lay eggs in them for one or two days. Then, the lid is placed on the container, closed tight, and put on a shelf at temperatures in the 80s (about 27°-30°C). About a week later the baby crickets will start hatching, at which point the lid is taken off and the containers are placed in a large aluminum box, which I use for breeding. The baby crickets are misted regularly and given fresh green weeds daily. I often use chickweed or clover.

Because my lizards all hibernate in winter, I have only three cricket containers in winter and cycle them so that in spring they start to lay eggs. In summer I then use 30 cricket boxes. I built my own cricket boxes with aluminum sheets; you can also use plastic storage boxes that are sold in department stores.

Warning: Crickets Bite!

When too many crickets are fed to small lizards inside a terrarium, they may start chewing on the toes or tails of sleeping lizards. It is even possible that the crickets could kill small lizards in the process, especially when they have nothing else to eat in the terrarium. Feed only as many crickets as your lizards will eat in a few minutes. Remove any excess.

Superworms

Superworms, *Zoophobas morio*, were originally found in caves in South America. Oilbirds brought food into these caves and dropped it on the floor, which started a food chain, in which superworms and six-spotted cockroaches are an important part. Coming from this environment, therefore, superworms and six-spotted roaches do not require light or high temperatures. They do well at temperatures in the mid- to upper 70s (about 22°-26°C). Superworms are actually the larva of a beetle, which is about an inch long and glossy black.

Young superworms should be given a bit of bran over the wood shavings in which they live. Once they are 3-4 weeks old, start feeding them potatoes, fruits, carrots, bread, cabbage, etc. The beetles are then given chicken food, dog food, pieces of fruit, and small bits of cat food. Again, superworms need to be gut-loaded a day or two prior to being fed to your lizards, and carrots and sweet potatoes are a good choice for that.

Breeding Superworms An important factor in breeding superworms is getting them to metamorphose into beetles. The larvae will not pupate if they are crowded. It's best to keep them separate, and cup them up one by one in a bit of slightly moist peat or old sawdust. After 3-4

Although they are omnivorous in nature, water dragons rarely eat plant matter in captivity. A sailfin lizard is on the right.

weeks at temperatures in the upper 70s (about 24°-26°C), you will have a beetle in every cup. When superworms escape inside the terrarium, they may also show up as beetles several weeks later because they can find good spots to pupate there. You can use the fact that larvae will not pupate when they are crowded to your advantage. Breed superworms in the summertime. Then store them over winter at temperatures in the 60s to low 70s (about 16°-23°C). The following spring and summer they are ready to be used as food, while you start breeding the superworms for the following year again.

For breeding, choose superworms that look very healthy. I keep 100 beetles per beetle cage, which is a one-eighth-inch (0.3 cm) screen cage. This cage sits on an aluminum tray, like those used for baking. A 1-inch (2.5 cm) thick layer of barely moist fine wood shavings or peat is put in the tray. The beetles will lay eggs through the screen into this layer of material. They will start laying eggs about three weeks after turning into beetles. Every week I replace the tray and wait a week for them to hatch. Then the aluminum trays are emptied into a larger tray. Therefore, you need two aluminum trays per beetle cage. One is below the cage for a week and the other is held for a week until the eggs hatch.

Six-Spotted Cockroaches

Six-spotted cockroaches, *Eublaberus distanti*, are often referred to as death's head cockroaches because they look very similar to *Blaberus craniifer*, having a vaguely skull-shaped mark on the back of the thorax. These six-spotted cockroaches are a good live food source for most lizards. They have many benefits compared to crickets, superworms, and other roaches:

Remember to Gut-load

Crickets, roaches, and mealworms should always be gut-loaded before being fed to your lizards. House them in a container with a highly nutritious diet for 24-48 hours before offering the prey to your water dragons. Several companies make insect gut-loads that you may want to try.

- They cannot climb smooth or almost smooth surfaces, and they stay inside feeder dishes.
- They do not require different cages for different age groups because all ages can live together. These roaches do not eat any live animals or their own babies. Because they will not try to eat any live animals, as crickets may do, they are also safe to keep in a terrarium in the event that they somehow manage to escape from the feeder dish. It is always possible that a lizard may grab a roach in the feeder dish and let if fall elsewhere, or more likely, that a water dragon's tail falls into the feeder dish and roaches climb up on it.
- All lizards seem to like these roaches.
- They are easy to gut-load with carotenes because they like to eat fruits and vegetables.
- All sizes of roaches are always available because the babies are very small when born. Therefore, by sifting through your supply you can sort out appropriately sized roaches for different–sized lizards.

The only disadvantage of this roach is its rather slow reproduction rate. You can overcome this by making large enclosures for them, which enables you to house hundreds of thousands. At night, when it is completely dark, the six-spotted cockroaches come to the surface in search of food: bran, bread, fruits, tomatoes, cantaloupes, potatoes, and even cabbage leaves. The substrate must be slightly moist, but not too wet. When you have many roaches and you feed them a lot of tomatoes, cantaloupes, watermelons, and other water rich food, the substrate will get too moist. This makes sifting them out a problem, and also the roaches will not thrive in it. Therefore, you need to adapt the type of food to the conditions needed. When the substrate is rather dry, give more fruit, and when the substrate gets too wet, start feeding more dry food like bread.

As substrate, old wood shavings or peat moss are useful. I have also found that these roaches live in loose black garden soil, but the disadvantage of soil is that it gets too heavy. Dead pulverized peat-like wood that you find inside a dead tree in the forest is an ideal substrate as well. You can use large plastic boxes to house the roaches.

Rodents

Rodents are excellent additional food for your water dragons. Breeding them is quite laborious, though. If you breed rodents, you must do this in a rodent escape-proof space. You can build an all-metal rat barn or buy a shed from a home improvement store. Escaped rats and mice will almost always cause problems in your house, garden, or in the terrariums. The rapid reproduction rate of rodents is well known.

My Start With Cockroaches

A decade ago, out of curiosity, I got my first six-spotted cockroaches from the Birmingham Zoo. I quickly realized that they were the ideal feeder insects for my lizards. I bred them for a few years without feeding any to my animals until I had hundreds of thousands. Now I have four containers filled with them. Each container is 7 feet (2.1 m) wide and 20 feet (6.1 m) long and the layer of substrate inside is over a foot (0.3 m) deep. I need them because I feed thousands of large lizards.

The Size of Food

The size of the food you feed your water dragons is very important. There are recommendations that the insects you feed your lizards should not be larger than the distance from eardrum to nostril. It is clear that in nature lizards don't measure insects before eating them. They simply eat what they can swallow, and if given the choice, will often choose the largest insect, which they can barely swallow. Nevertheless, people have come up with the idea that feeder insects should always be smaller than a certain size.

Why did they come up with this strange idea? The reasoning could be as follows. When lizards are kept indoors, they sometimes do not get enough UVB light (see the section on UVB light in the Chapter 2). In addition, there may not be enough calcium in the food they are eating. Also, if

Various species of roaches are available from online suppliers, and they make an excellent food for water dragons.

the babies are raised in the same way as their parents, they also receive insufficient amounts of UVB light and/or calcium. As a result, they will have difficulty feeding.

In a lizard's attempt to eat a large insect, as may occur in nature, he would choke because it would get stuck halfway down the throat. When the lizard dies, the owner concludes that it was because the prey was too large. However, the real cause was not the size of the insect, but the fact that the animal's weakened muscles and bones did not assist the animal in swallowing properly, which in turn was a result if improper care. This highlights the importance of ensuring your lizard receives adequate calcium and UVB light, and not to try to get around it by feeding him smaller insects.

Chapter 4

Health Care

S tressful conditions, improper housing, and
substandard food are the main causes for
health problems and diseases in water
dragons. The conscientious hobbyist should
learn the normal appearance and behavior
of his or her pet and act quickly if anything
changes. Although it is useful for hobbyists to be
able to recognize specific illnesses, it is more
important to know your pet well and realize when
it is acting abnormally.

Veterinary Care

Taking your newly purchased lizard for a visit to the veterinarian is always a good idea. That way, you can get an idea if parasites are present. Many parasites are quite common and are of no direct danger to your lizard, so you do not need to panic if parasites are found. Unfortunately, most people only start thinking about visiting a vet when the lizard is already irreversibly ill. Lizards do not show signs that they are ill until they are very ill. Therefore, you need to watch for slight changes in appetite, behavior, etc. Once your lizard is visibly ill, which means he is usually lying in the corner with his eyes closed, a visit to the vet will likely not help. In that case, you cannot blame him if the animal dies under his care because you detected the illness too late. Also, the very handling of the sick animal will most likely speed up the disease and make him die faster, as this kind of handling is very stressful for a lizard that is too sick to move away from danger.

In the US, there are some exceptionally good reptile veterinarians, but most people will not easily locate one in their home areas. This being the case, it is best to be prepared and establish a good relationship with a local vet before your lizard becomes sick. If you do some research, you will likely find someone qualified near your town.

Skin Problems
Shedding Difficulty

Shedding problems (called *dysecdysis*) occur when lizards are kept too dry. You will notice that not all of the skin will shed and that, especially on the toes and tail tip, bits of skin will remain. These remnants will become a breeding ground for bacteria, and eventually toes can become infected and fall off. Heated terraria may often be too dry, and if no preventative steps are taken, this condition will almost always lead to shedding problems. The easiest way to avoid this situation is to provide the lizards with moist hiding places. They will spend

Observing your dragon daily gives you the best chance to discover an illness before it becomes serious.

a lot of time in these areas so that their skin can soak up needed moisture. Even a ten-minute misting will not be adequate in this circumstance.

Blisters

If your water dragons are kept excessively moist all the time and if dry warm basking places are lacking, they will develop blisters. Initially, they may appear on the belly, where you may not recognize the problem in time to prevent serious infection. In the case of Australian water dragons, blisters can also start during hibernation in winter, but these blisters should go away after one or two sheddings in the springtime.

If kept excessively wet, water dragons will develop blisters (circled in red)

Most blisters can be cured quite easily if detected early enough, but the animals should be kept in a proper habitat in the first place to prevent this from occurring at all. If this should happen, you can try putting some antibacterial ointment or 2 percent chlorhexidine solution on the blisters, but keep it away from the eyes and mouth. Also, you can apply foot rot and ringworm spray used

Signs of an Unhealthy Dragon

If your water dragon displays any of the signs in the list below, it may need veterinary attention. If you are in doubt, it is better to seek the opinion of a veterinarian with experience in reptile medicine than to wait and see what happens. The sooner the animal sees the vet, the greater the chance it will recover.

- **abnormal feces—runny, odd color, excessive odor, worms**
- **inability to right itself when turned upside down**
- **limping or dragging a limb**
- **listless or sluggish behavior—can be caused by cool temperatures**
- **refusing food—can be caused by temperature extremes**
- **sunken eyes**
- **vomiting**
- **weight loss**

for cattle to the area. However, if you do not see improvement within a few days, you must consult your veterinarian, who will able to determine the exact bacteria or fungus causing the blisters so that you can more adequately treat the animal.

Vitamin A Deficiency

Often, captive lizards lack vitamin A or carotenes, which are the naturally occurring precursors to vitamin A. Lizard species, like water dragons, that normally live in natural habitats full of green leaves are not usually susceptible to this deficiency. The green leaves are a source of carotenes, and lizards living in such a green environment will routinely consume insects with remnants of these green leaves in their guts.

When lizards are fed insects in captivity, you need to make sure that these feeder insects contain enough carotenes. Alas, often that is not the case. Feeder insects are not always gut loaded properly. A lack of carotenes will result in a lack of vitamin A, which will make the water dragons more vulnerable to parasites and infections because their immune systems are weakened. Watery eyes are usually the first visible sign of a weakened immune system, particularly if there is too much dry dust inside the terrarium.

In nature, water dragons almost never have direct access to vitamin A because insects have no liver in which this vitamin is usually stored. Therefore, it is best to avoid direct use of vitamin A, because an overdose of this vitamin is toxic both to animals and people. In the case of an overdose, your animal may develop a swollen throat. Unfortunately, this remains poorly understood as some powders used to dust insects still contain vitamin A. You should avoid supplementing vitamin A, but be sure to feed your lizards enough carotenes in the form that they appear in nature, such as gut-loaded insects and leaves.

Metabolic Bone Disease

Metabolic bone disease (MBD) is most often caused by a lack of direct sunlight or a lack of UVB. It can also be caused by a lack of calcium in the food source. Therefore, the proper amount of exposure to UVB and sun is the most important factor in avoiding MBD. When water dragons are kept indoors, people use UVB lights that emit less— often much less— UVB than the sun, but compensate by dusting plenty of calcium on feeder insects. To enable them to digest calcium from their food, vitamin D3 is needed. In nature, water dragons receive vitamin D3 by exposing their skin to direct sunlight. Direct sunlight means that it is not filtered by glass or plastic, as most glass and plastic will filter out almost all of the needed UVB light.

If you are not able to give your lizards access to direct sunlight, you have to look into the use of UVB lights that are made especially for them. In the past, people mainly depended on florescent tubes for that because bulbs were only made for very large enclosures. Nowadays, smaller bulbs are also made for that purpose. They may cost more, but may last longer as well. The proper use of a good brand of UVB light can be a bit difficult. You will need to read the instructions to calculate proper placement, as the distance to the UVB light is an important factor. For most bulbs, you dragon must be able to get within a foot (30.5 cm) of the bulb. UV lights are discussed in more detail in Chapter 2. Also, the time that the light is on, or the time that the lizards actually spend under that light is important to their well-being.

Note the damaged snout of this water dragon. These lizards are notorious for running smack into the terrarium glass.

Lizards that lack calcium will not only develop soft bones that break easily, but will also get cramps due to a shortage of calcium in their muscles. You will usually see these lizards shaking or their legs cramping. If the lizard gets to this point, a veterinarian will usually give him a calcium-gluconate injection to boost his calcium levels. Additionally, habitat conditions should be changed, and you will need to provide better UVB light or sun and add more calcium to his diet.

Nose Bouncers

Water dragons, and especially green water dragons, are sometimes known

Handling

The handling of a lizard is something that is best avoided. In the first place, lizards do not like it. Even long-term captive bearded dragons do not like it. This has been scientifically proven recently (Miller, K. et al, 2004). At best, they will tolerate it, but it causes stress, which weakens the immune system. Also, handling can transport parasites from one animal to another and can also transport some pathogens to you. Most pet keepers do want to handle their lizards, however. When you handle your dragon, do so only for short periods of time and wash your hands thoroughly before and after.

as "nose bouncers." Water dragons do not know that they cannot walk through glass. They can see through it, so they believe that they can walk or even run through it. When startled, they will run headlong into the glass, sometimes causing serious trauma to the snout. If the snout is bleeding or misshapen, immediate vet care is needed.

This situation needs to be avoided, because an injured nose is unlikely to heal completely. Once the animal is damaged, he will stay damaged. A terrarium for water dragons must have as little glass as possible. The back and sides must be of a nontransparent material. The front can be glass, but it is better if the lowest third also be made of nontransparent material. If you are using a glass enclosure, you should paint or cover these areas, so your dragon will know there is a barrier.

Injuries

For injuries from bites to broken tails, you can try using a medicinal healing powder like the one used on horses. Among other things, it contains activated charcoal which dries out the wound rapidly. An injured water dragon should only be given a small water dish for drinking, so that he will not wash away the powder during bathing. Especially in an outdoor habitat, it is important to have the wound dry out fast so that flies will not lay their eggs there. You can also use human triple antibiotic ointment, which many hobbyist have used with good success.

Heat Stress

When your water dragon's terrarium accidentally reaches too high a temperature, the animal may become listless and its muscles will no longer function properly. When handled, the animal may feel limp and lifeless but is still alive. If that happens, you need to immediately put the water dragon under the tap and have cool—not cold—water run over his body. If several water dragons have this problem, spray cool water over them with a mister.

Egg Binding

Egg binding, also called *dystocia*, is a condition in which an animal cannot lay its eggs. It is a serious problem and may be fatal in only a few days. Like most health issues in reptiles, egg-binding is easier to prevent than cure.

A water dragon can get egg bound for several reasons. In nature, female water dragons and many other lizards need to find a safe place to lay eggs. Along with being a place suitable for eggs to develop (like correct substrate or good exposure to sunlight), it should also be a quiet and safe place. The female will spend about an hour or more digging the burrow in which to lay the eggs. This makes her very vulnerable to predators. Therefore, when lizards are in a terrarium, they will also look for these conditions. Often they are not present, so the female keeps looking. But during this time the eggs will grow too big to be laid. The female is then egg bound.

It is best to handle water dragons only when necessary; frequent handling can cause them stress.

Another reason for becoming egg bound is that the female's muscles and skeleton may be too weak to lay the eggs. The developing eggs will demand calcium from the body of the lizard, and if not enough UVB or sunlight was provided, the female will be lacking calcium in her body before fully developing the eggs. In some cases, an egg is deformed and obstructs the passage of other eggs.

Sometimes an injection of calcium-gluconate can help. Hormones that work well for turtles for the deposition of the eggs mostly do not work for lizards. Prevention is almost the only solution. When there is a gravid lizard in the terrarium, make sure to give her enough UVB light, excellent food, and provide her with a few choices of sites to lay her eggs. See Chapter 6 for instructions on constructing a nest site.

Chapter 5

Green Water Dragons

The green water dragon is the most popular of the lizards discussed in this book. Thousands of them are imported into the US and Europe every year, mostly from Vietnam. Chances are that the first water dragon you ever saw was an imported hatchling in a pet store.

Range

The green water dragon is found on continental Southeast Asia. To the west of the continent, the species lives in the larger part of Myanmar (Burma), but is not found in the northern third or on the southern peninsula of that country. In southern China, the green water dragon is found roughly south of the tropic of Cancer in three provinces: Yunnan, Guangdong, and Guangxi (Zhao and Adler, 1993). The species is found in all of former Indochina, which today comprises Vietnam, Cambodia, and Laos. It also lives in the biggest part of Thailand, except on the southern peninsula, where its range ends at about a 13 degree northern latitude. This species is not present in the Malayan Peninsula or Indonesia.

Habitat

Green water dragons are most often found in tropical lowland forest. In Vietnam, they have been found at elevations between 300 and 1000 feet (about 91-305 m) (Tomey, 1985; Manthey and Manthey, 2000), and in Laos they have been found at elevations between 200 and 2300 feet (about 61-701 m) (Stuart, 1999). In Thailand's national park, Khao Yai, about 110 miles (about 161 km) northeast of Bangkok, green water dragons have been found at an elevation of 2300 feet (about 701 m).

They are always found in proximity to water, such as a river, brook, or pond. Green water dragons sleep on branches over bodies of water. In case of danger, they can let themselves fall off the branches and hide under the water. These animals do not always choose to hide in water, however. Manthey and Manthey

The green water dragon is a common lizard in the forests of China and Southeast Asia.

(1999) noticed that lizards close to the side of the river repeatedly preferred to hide on land between bushes and in crevices between rocks. For egg deposition, they use sandy areas, which will also be present in their habitats.

Climate

Mengzi in southern China is at the northern limit of the range of this species. Here, night frosts are possible in winter. With captive-bred green water dragons, temperatures below 42°F (5.6°C) can be lethal. Either the captive animals I have worked with were from

Climate for January and July in the Range of the Green Water Dragon

JANUARY

	AD Min	AD Max	HR	LR	%RH (10 am- 4 pm)	AMP
Hanoi	56°F (13.3°C)	68°F (20C)	92°F (33.3°C)	42°F (5.5°C)	78% - 68% 78% - 68%	0.7 inches (1.8 cm)
Vientiane	57°F (13.9°C)	83°F (28.3°C)	95°F (35°C)	39°F (3.9°C)	77% 77%	0.2 inches (0.5 cm)
Bangkok	68°F (20°C)	89°F (31.7°C)	100°F (37.8°C)	55°F (12.8°C)	91%-53% 91%-53%	0.3 inches (0.8 cm)
Phnom Penh	70°F (21.1°C)	87°F (30.6°C)	96°F (35.6°C)	57°F (13.9°C)	71% 71%	0.3 inches (0.8 cm)
Mengzi	46°F (7.8°C)	68°F (20°C)	84°F (28.9°C)	29°F (-1.7°C)	55% 55%	0.3 inches (0.8 cm)

JULY

	AD Min	AD Max	HR	LR	%RH (10 am- 4 pm)	AMP
Hanoi	78°F (25.6°C)	91°F (32.8°C)	104°F (40°C)	71°F (21.7°C)	79%-72% 79%-72%	12.7 inches (32.2 cm)
Vientiane	75°F (23.9°C)	87°F (30.6°C)	94°F (34.4°C)	70°F (21.1°C)	87% 87%	10.5 inches (26.7 cm)
Bangkok	76°F) (24.4°C)	90°F 32.2°C)	101°F (38.3°C)	71°F (21.7°C)	91%-66% 91%-66%	6.3 inches (16 cm)
Phnom Penh	75°F (23.9°C)	F89°F (31.7°C)	98°F (36.7°C)	68°F (20°C)	83% 83%	6.7 inches (17 cm)
Mengzi	67°F (19.4°C)	83°F (28.3°C)	95°F (35°C)	59°F (15°C)	69% 69%	7.7 inches (19.6 cm)

Key: AD=average daily temperature; HR=highest recorded temperature; LR=lowest recorded temperature; RH=relative humidity; AMP=average monthly precipitation

warmer, more southern regions of their range, or the animals at the northern edge of the range avoid being overcome by seeking shelter during cold nights in places where the temperatures stay high enough for survival. It is plausible that in comparable climates, like Miami for example, tropical reptiles can survive night frosts by finding warmer hiding places. Cold spells there are very short and therefore the temperature stays high enough that the animals would be warm in burrows in the ground. From the table showing the green water dragon's climate range, you also see that extremes over 100°F (37.8°C) are very rare or nonexistent.

Everywhere within the range of the green water dragon you see a well-defined dry period from November to March and a rainy period from May to September. These existing dry and wet seasons may very well trigger reproduction. Manthey and Manthey (1999/2000) found eggs in nests at sandy beaches at the end of the dry season in Laos, March to May. The babies from such nests will hatch in the wet season (when presumably food is most available), which makes laying eggs during the last six or seven weeks of the dry season favorable for reproduction.

SVL

One measurement used often in herpetology is the snout-to-vent length, or SVL. This is the length of an animal measured from tip of the nose across the belly to the cloaca, or vent. It excludes the tail. The reason the tail is excluded is that so many lizards (and to a lesser extent snakes and salamanders) lose their tails that including the tail length often gives an inaccurate impression of the animal's true size and possibly age.

Description
Size

These impressive lizards reach an average total length of 24 inches (about 61 cm), but maximum sizes of 30-32 inches (about 76-81cm) are possible. Guard and Strimple (1998) even mention a maximum total length of 38 inches (96.5 cm). The tail length is about two-thirds of the total body length. In Laos, Manthey and Manthey (1999/2000) found a female of record size: the SVL (snout-vent length) was nearly 9 inches and the tail length was over 20 inches (225 mm, 515 mm respectively to be exact).

Body

The head is large and square. On the neck, there is a ridge in the longitudinal direction, called the *nuchal crest*. On top of this nuchal crest there are a few spines. Over the top of the back, these spines continue until the middle of the tail. This row of spines is only interrupted at the start of the tail. Males have long triangular spines. As they grow older, these spines will grow longer and can reach a length of about half an inch (1.27 cm). In females, these spines are also present, but they are smaller.

Between these spines are smaller scales on the head and the back. The spines, which are on top of the beginning of the tail, are not interrupted by smaller scales. Toward the middle of the tail, the spines disappear and make room for a double row of enlarged scales that continue to end of the tail. The body and tail are slightly flattened in a vertical direction, especially at the beginning of the tail.

On the cheeks and lower jaw area, there are enlarged scales that often form cones. These enlarged scales are white or pinkish in color. The rostral scale at the tip of the mouth is a little wider than it is high. The rear side of this rostral is bordered by eight postrostral scales. These postrostral scales are between two supralabial scales, one at each side. Around the mouth are 12-14 supralabial scales and 10-12 infralabial scales. Along the lower jaw are two rows of enlarged scales that start at the chin. Above the supralabial scales is also a row of enlarged scales.

Adult green water dragons have enlarged conical scales on their puffy jowls.

Between the nostril and the rostral scale are three scales and between the nostril and supralabial scales are five scales. Around the nostril is a ring consisting of slightly protruding scales. Below the eye is a line of four to six enlarged subocular scales. On each side is a row of four to eight femoral pores. The body scales are small. The ventral scales are larger than the dorsal scales. The dorsal scales are keeled, and these keels get gradually weaker and disappear toward the sides of the body. The dorsal scales are a bit larger near the middle of the back. The ventral scales are not keeled, but the subcaudal scales are keeled too, especially under the first quarter of the tail. There is no dewlap, unlike in iguanas.

Scale Terms

The various scales on lizards have been given names to facilitate biological discussions. These names are often used by hobbyists. A glossary of some of those terms is below.

- **dorsal: scales on the back of the lizard.**
- **infralabial: scale on the border of the lower "lip" (although lizards don't really have lips).**
- **postrostral: scales in contact with the posterior edge of the rostral scale.**
- **rostral: scale on the tip of the snout.**
- **subcaudal: scales on the underside of the tail.**
- **subocular: scales right below the eye.**
- **supralabial: scales on the upper "lip."**
- **ventral: scales on the underside of the lizard.**

Coloration

The basic coloration of this species is green with various shades ranging from olive green to bluish green. Green water dragons that are kept indoors for a long period will gradually loose their beautiful green coloration, which will fade to bluish gray. The exact cause of this is not known, but it seems that lack of sunlight causes this problem, even though the animals are kept under UVB light. Therefore, if at all possible, you must place the terrarium in a location where the sun can shine in at least part of the day—although remember to not let sunlight shine into a glass enclosure.

The young animals have three to five, light-colored, oblique stripes on each side. These stripes are still present in the adults, but are much less clearly visible. The babies also have relatively larger heads than the adults. Where the crest will later grow, there are only enlarged scales. The babies are also darker colored than the adults. Their coloration is more olive brown with a hint of green. The tail has dark and light brown rings around it.

The top of the water dragon's head is somewhat darker colored. This is especially true in older males. Often, there is a dark band visible on the side of the head from eye to ear opening, particularly in older males. The enlarged scales of the lower jaw are white, pinkish white, bluish white, or even orange colored.

Many males have a yellow to orange colored area behind their front legs. The throat and front belly are whitish to green, but can also be yellow to orange colored. According to Taylor (1963), the belly can have bluish dots on it. The last three-quarters of the tail has darker colored bands around it. These dark bands get more dominating toward the tip of the tail and reduce the green color there to dots. At lower temperatures, the green water dragons

Green water dragons, especially males, develop impressive crests on the neck, back, and tail as they age.

get darker. Young green water dragons are more brown and olive colored.

Diet

In nature, the main food source for green water dragons is insects and other invertebrates. Ziegler (2002) studied the stomach contents of 28 water dragons in Vietnam. Most frequently, he found beetles in the greatest abundance, followed by grasshoppers and their kin, spiders, and millipedes (also a centipede and a blind snake). Jauch (1979) described how his water dragons liked to catch crickets that were thrown in the water. They would dive in and catch them while swimming. Also Smith (1935) and Tomey (1985) described how, in nature, water dragons would catch insects that were floating on the water surface. They also state that the dragons would catch fish in the water.

Ziegler (2002) found that one-third of the food that was inside the well-filled stomach

and
intestines
of the 28
water dragons they
researched consisted of
plant material. Older animals
had relatively more plant material
in their stomachs and intestines. The
oldest water dragons had up to 80-90 percent
plant material in their food. These results are quite
amazing, because water dragons often refuse to eat plant
material in captivity.

Mature male green water dragons often have a peach-colored patch behind the front legs.

One explanation could be that the Ziegler's research refers only to one place and one period in Vietnam. Another explanation could be that animals in captivity get plenty of insects and small vertebrates, which very well may be a preferred food in nature as well. It is possible that in nature they do not find enough of their preferred food and will have to rely more on plant material. It's almost like spoiled children that do not want to eat their vegetables when they are going to get ice cream, etc. It is, therefore, necessary to provide sufficient greens to the feeder insects in case the water dragons refuse to eat plant material.

Werning (2002) lists the following food items that were accepted by his water dragons in captivity: various species of crickets, locusts, grasshoppers, butterflies, moths, cockroaches, and insect larvae like mealworms, wax moth larvae, and superworms. They also ate beetles like mealworm beetles and even superworm beetles (*Zoophobas morio*), small lizards (even their own young), earthworms, mice, young rats, fish, fresh water crabs (*Potamon*), mussels, small birds, tarantulas (*Eurypelma*), meat, frogs, snakes (*Natrix natrix*), bananas, grapes, tomatoes, oranges, apples, strawberries, cantaloupes, melons, lettuce, dandelion, chicory, cauliflower, brussels sprouts, chickweeds, cooked carrots, cooked rice, plums, cherries, and milk powder.

Individual water dragons may refuse certain types of the above-mentioned food. Werning wrote that some of his animals never accepted mice, while others never accepted any vegetarian food. Therefore, you need to determine by trial and error what your animals are eating and what they will refuse as food. Also, Mader (1994) wrote that water dragons may refuse to eat the chopped fruits and vegetables you prepare for them. He fed his animals the following with success: adult mice, fish (large comets), day-old quail chicks, earthworms, and the occasional bugs that entered the terrariums. He gave an adult mouse to each female every week, and the males received one or two mice every week, depending on their appetite. Fish were always present in the water pan. Every third week chicks were fed instead of mice. The food was always dusted with a commercial vitamin/mineral supplement once per week.

Reproduction
Sexing

In adult animals, the males and females are easily distinguished. The males have larger crests, bigger heads, more pronounced cheeks, and heavier bodies. They often have an

Sexing at a Glance

Male	Female
large cheeks	small cheeks
large nuchal and dorsal crests	small nuchal and dorsal crests
large head	small head
swelling at base of tail	no swelling at base of tail
prominent femoral pores	inconspicuous femoral pores
often have orange color behind front legs	no orange color behind front legs
pinkish or bluish lips and/or cheeks	no pink or blue on lips and cheeks

orange-colored area behind the front legs, a darker chin, and pinkish or bluish colors on the cheeks. The males also have a wider tail root and better developed femoral pores (pores on the undersides of the thighs) than the females.

In younger animals, the sexes cannot be recognized in a definite way. In a group of growing young animals, males can tentatively be recognized as having a faster rate of growth and crest development than the others. But growing green water dragons that appear to be females may very well be suppressed males. Therefore, it is always unclear which sex the animal actually is at this stage (Werning, 2002). Probing is not a reliable way to determine the sex of the animal. Muscle contractions in the area can strongly influence the depth of the entering probe. Furthermore, the risk of damaging the animals in the process should not be underestimated.

Personal Experience

In 1989, I received a few animals from the National Zoo in Washington, DC, to try to breed. In 1990, these animals produced four babies that hatched on September 21st and

Green water dragons should be kept in colonies of one male and one or more females for breeding purposes. The bluish lizard in front is the male.

September 23rd. The eggs were laid on July 17th, so that the incubation time was 66-68 days at an incubation temperature of about 82°F (27.8°C).

In 1991, the animals again produced four babies that hatched on September 12th and September 13th. The exact date of egg deposition is

When keeping water dragons in groups, keep a careful eye out for any aggression between the lizards.

unknown, but was probably during the first half of July. These green water dragons were kept outdoors from mid-April to mid-October, and were moved to indoor terrraria during the colder six months. Successful breeding, therefore, only took place in the middle of the warm period, when the animals were kept outdoors. Around this time, I was trying to find more cold-tolerant green water dragons from regions in southern China at the northern limits of their range, but could not do so. In early 1991, I was fortunate to be able to receive a number of zoo-bred Australian water dragons and shifted my breeding attempts to them.

Aggression and Social Behavior

There are a number of people that have successfully bred green water dragons and published their findings. Mader (1994) describes the captive breeding of green water dragons. He suggests keeping a breeding colony in a large enclosure. The colony should consist of one male and one or more females. Although two males may (or may not) tolerate each other in a larger enclosure, it is better to have just one male, because the tension caused by repeated confrontations will cause stress, even if you do not notice any fighting. This stress can weaken the animals' defenses against parasites and thus hinder successful reproduction and cause their health to deteriorate. On the other hand, there is always the risk of having an infertile male. So, if you have an extra male, you can exchange males if all your females lay infertile eggs with the first male.

When you are breeding with only one pair of water dragons, you must be aware that the female cannot get away from the male. Sometimes an overactive male may copulate so often with the female that she will get numerous bite wounds in the neck area. If that occurs, it is best to keep both animals separate for awhile until the wounds are healed.

Especially during the breeding season, females can show aggression toward each other. With Australian water dragons, females have been known to chase each other away from the best egg deposition site. The same thing can be expected with green water dragons. Therefore, you need to watch out for aggression between females as well as males. To reduce the problem, you must try to keep only similarly sized females together, otherwise the smaller younger females will always be chased away and may eventually die. You can look for scars, especially at the tail tip, because aggressive female Australian water dragons tend to bite each other's tail tips off. It's also likely that green water dragon females will do the same. Also watch for head bobbing among the larger females and waving of the front legs of the smaller females.

Female green water dragons will make their nests in damp sand.

Because the animals will act differently when you are present, you can use a camcorder to check for mutual aggression. Have it run for two hours when no one is present in the room and then check later to see what happened during that period.

Environmental Conditions

The climate in the range of the green water dragon has a dry season and a wet season, and it is very likely that the change of these seasons will trigger breeding. In Laos, freshly laid eggs were found toward the end of the dry season (Manthey and Manthey, 1999/2000). These nests were 4 inches wide (10.2 cm) and almost 5 inches (12.7 cm) deep. One nest contained 12 eggs and the other nest contained 15 eggs. The eggs from these nests hatched at the start of the rainy season, when more food was present for the babies. The mating must have occurred about two months prior to egg deposition, which would be around January or February. In Laos, November, December, January, and February are the four driest months of the year, while most rain falls from May through September. Dr. Mader, who lives in Florida, writes that all the eggs of his green water dragons were laid from December to March, which is also the dry season in Florida. K. Ullrich (1979) had

nests all year round in his indoor terrarium. He kept them at 82°-84°F (27.8-28.9°C) and a bit warmer in winter. He describes 11 nests: two nests had 8 eggs, two nests had 9 eggs, two nests had 10 eggs, 4 had 11 eggs, and 1 had 16 eggs. The nests were found in the months January, February, March, April, May, July, August, October, November, and December.

Nesting

While researching these animals, Manthey and Manthey (1999) observed that local people collected lizard eggs for consumption. This occurred in the Phou Khao Kouay National Park of Laos, about 70 miles (about 113 km) southeast of Vientiane. They found two nests that had eggs in them, 12 in one nest and 15 in the other. As these nests were not well covered, the eggs on top had already dried out. At the side of a nest, they found one egg. The female must have been disturbed by egg collectors and laid an egg while running away. After Manthey and Manthey dug the eggs deeper into the nest so they were covered properly, they realized that they, too, were later dug up by egg collectors. The females apparently always come back to the same sandy areas to lay their eggs, so collecting them was not difficult. They found 15 sites close together in that locale. These eggs were laid between some flat rocks

Egg Size

The size of the eggs can vary; the smallest eggs recorded were 20 x 10 mm and 2.5 grams and the biggest eggs were 28 x 16 mm and 3.4 grams (one inch = 25.4 mm) Near the moment of hatching, they are between 30 x 22 mm and 40 x 30 mm (Werning, 2002).

not far from the river. Collectors had already emptied most of the nests. This means that within a few days time at least 15 females had come there to deposit their eggs. However, the green water dragon population did not (yet) seem to suffer from this practice.

The female will dig a burrow in sandy soil, and when that burrow is deep enough she will lay her eggs and cover the burrow again. Schliemann (1968) describes how the female digs her nest. First, she will start digging one side of the nest, and then she will turn around 180 degrees and burrow the other side of the nest. When the nest is deep enough (4 to 10 inches (10.2-25.4 cm) was registered in captivity), she will turn around, lift up her tail, and start laying her eggs. The egg deposition lasts about half an hour. The number of eggs per clutch generally ranges from 7 to 12. Kammerer (1999) describes clutches of up to 23 eggs. Werning

(2002) found the smallest clutch he recorded was four eggs from a young female. He also wrote that his 18-year-old female is still laying one or two clutches of eggs every year, but since she was 14 years old these nests have consisted of only five to seven eggs.

Werning (2002), who bred green water dragons for many years, never found any indication that TDST (temperature dependant sex determination) exists in this species, such as in the case of Australian water dragons.

Incubation

Eggs can be successfully incubated in moist, coarse vermiculate. A higher temperature tends to produce a shorter incubation period, but be careful that you do not keep the eggs too warm. At a steady 86°F (30°C) in moist vermiculate, Mader's females hatched eggs after about 65 days. The vermiculite was kept moist all the time. The incubation periods found in the literature vary between 60 and 99 days.

I have bred 150 species of reptiles since 1970, and my personal observation is that when the incubation lasted longer than normal, the babies, as a rule, were smaller and weaker as well. It is quite possible that when not enough ingredients for normal growth of the embryo are present in the eggs, the embryo will have to grow at a slower pace. Therefore, if you see that incubation periods are too long, you need to address this by giving the egg-laying females better food and overall conditions.

Keeping this in mind, it may very well be that the incubation period in nature can be shorter than the above-mentioned lower limit of 60 days, because in nature the female has a better chance of finding the necessary food and living conditions. Because females tend to protect their nests for a day or more against other nesting females, it may be better to wait a period of one or two days before removing the eggs for incubation.

The findings of Manthey and Manthey suggest that the eggs can be rather dry at the start of the incubation period, as they found eggs during the dry season in Laos. Some eggs were even shrunken a bit as a result of the rather dry sand in which they were found. It seems that the rainy season will also stimulate and help the babies to hatch because the sand will

Get Ready to Incubate

It is recommended that you have the incubator set up for at least several days before you think you will need it. By doing this, you can make sure the incubator is holding the correct temperature without exposing the eggs to temperature fluctuations while you adjust the thermostat. Also, if your dragon happens to lay eggs earlier than predicted, you will be ready.

Sperm Retention

In many species of reptiles, the females can save sperm from mating and use it to fertilize future eggs, sometimes years after the original mating. The de Bitters (1986) describe a rather interesting story about sperm saving green water dragons. They had a male and two female green water dragons. All were adults. In June 1983 the male died. Amazingly, the two females copulated on January 30th 1985. The copulation looked like a real copulation with neck biting of the smaller female and cloacas touching for two minutes. The terrarium contained a bucket of sand for possible egg deposition. On March 20th 1985, or about 50 days after the pseudo-copulation, one of the two females laid eggs in the bucket, whereupon the bucket was taken out to remove the eggs for incubation. The next day, the bucket was placed back again, and immediately the other female laid eggs in the bucket. Although the eggs did not hatch, embryos were found in the eggs of the clutches of both females! Also, Kammerer (1999) writes how a female that did not have contact with a male for 18 months laid a clutch of eggs of which at least one was fertile.

be soaked with rainwater. In captive breeding, this translates into keeping the substrate in which the eggs incubate moister toward the end of the incubation period.

When eggs are fertile and healthy, they will increase in size during incubation. Due to osmosis the inside pressure is quite high, so the eggs should feel hard and sturdy when you press gently on them with your fingertips. When eggs feel soft—and when this is not a result of dry conditions—they are most often dead. Although I have seen healthy eggs develop well alongside these eggs, it seems better to remove dead eggs from the incubator.

When eggs die during incubation, most people tend to blame it on improper methods of incubation. Of course, it is possible to incubate eggs the wrong way, but more often there is another cause for this. The tiny embryos need many elements to grow strong and healthy. They get this food from the mother animal. If she did not receive all the necessary food elements or UVB light, there will be a shortage of something inside the egg. In most cases, it's probably calcium. Eggs that do not contain enough calcium or other elements will grow at first, but then will die off when the supply runs out. Often, embryos will develop all the way to the moment of hatching and then die. When you open these eggs you will see completely developed baby water dragons. Apparently, this is caused by the fact that these babies were not able to escape from the egg. It can be that the skin of the egg was too hard or too dry. Therefore, it is necessary to keep the eggs a bit more moist toward the end of the incubation.

Other babies that cannot hatch may have had muscles or bones that were too weak to enable them to make it out of the eggs. If it appears that most embryos have already died, you can try to open the remaining eggs carefully and see if the babies escape. However, you need to realize that such babies are often very weak and most likely will die soon. With intense care, you may be able to save a baby or two. However, it's better to prevent this by giving the female enough sun, UVB light, calcium, and good varied food. Stress is also a negative factor. It opens the way for intestinal diseases (and other illnesses), which will impair proper working of the intestines so that important food elements will pass through without being used by the female. When females double clutch, it occasionally happens that most eggs of the first clutch hatch, while the eggs of the second clutch die off. This is a sign that the female ran out of her reserves when producing the first clutch.

Although you can keep hatchling water dragons in groups, be careful to not overcrowd them.

The dark hatchling is melanistic, meaning it produces excessive dark skin pigments.

Most people incubate at a steady temperature, but you need to keep in mind that this is not the case in nature. It may, therefore, be better for the development of the embryos to allow for a slight cooling of the eggs at night, say to 80°F (26.7°C), and return to around 85°F (29.4°C) during the day. With Australian water dragons, it's been found that, at a lower nighttime incubation temperature, all babies will hatch within a two to three hour time frame during the day. Although this has never been researched for green water dragons, it's expected that their babies will hatch in the early morning also.

Hatchlings and Hatchling Care

Hatchlings are about 5-6 inches (about 12.7-15.2 cm), of which one-quarter of the length is SVL. Werning (2002) writes that newly hatched babies can be up to 16.5 cm, which is about 6.5 inches.

Dedekind and Petzold (1982) noticed in one case that, about three weeks before hatching, the female was almost constantly in the neighborhood of the nest. She went into the water more often and returned to put her wet dripping body on top of the screen that covered the nest, as if she were moistening the eggs. This may be a coincidence, but it may also be a sign that the female is watching, protecting, and even moistening the nest during the period a few weeks prior to hatching. Because most breeders remove the eggs for incubation, such observations are not possible in most situations. I keep hundreds of adult breeding female Australian water dragon and never made such an observation. I also remove the eggs for incubation, as newborn babies would be able to escape through narrow openings. But I never saw a female more in one place than another, but I may not have observed well enough. For now, all you can do is allow for the possibility that a female guards her nest at the end of the incubation period.

Green water dragon babies can be raised in rather small enclosures at the start, but avoid keeping too many together. In the hatchling enclosures, the babies should have branches and twigs to climb on. The water bowl must be easy to get out of and must either be shallow or have rough sides or edges. Another way to help the babies leave the water bowl is by putting some pieces of wood or twigs in the water on which they can climb out.

When you clean the water, you need to take care that the temperature of the water is appropriate. Feel the temperature of the tap water with your fingers. It should be somewhere between 70° and 85°F (about 21°-29°C). Although I have seen Australian water dragons survive in cold water under a thin layer of ice, green water dragons would die below 42°F (5.5°C). However, water that is 50° to 60°F (about 10°-15.6°C) is too cold too, because it will give them muscle cramps and they may then die from drowning.

Baby water dragons will also need UVB light. Sun is always the best, and if sunshine is not possible, you should buy a UVB light that is designed for lizards. Feeder insects need to contain all the necessary nutritional ingredients to make them grow healthy and strong. The simplest way to do this is by gut-loading the feeder insects with a variety of food, because the water dragons will eat the insects along with the food that is in their digestive tract. You need to make sure that enough calcium and carotenes are present in the insects.

Air humidity should be correct—higher at night and in the morning, as in nature. Constant dryness will result in shedding problems, while constant wet conditions will cause skin problems and blisters. The baby water dragons should feel as safe as possible, which means that handling should be avoided and hiding places provided. Stressed animals will get weakened defense systems or may refuse to eat.

In four to eight weeks, the babies will shed for the first time. According to Werning (2002), the males will grow faster in the first six months; their heads and cheeks will get larger. At this point, the males can grow to about 14-16 inches (about 36-41 cm) total length, while females will not yet have reached 12 inches (about 31 cm). Six-month old males can be twice as heavy as females of the same age. This is when the first conflicts between the males begin.

If you rear your babies in the correct way, you will need to place them in a larger tank after about six months. They should reach adult size in two to three years. At the age of one year, the young ones should reach 20-24 inches (about 51-61 cm), if they are well fed.

Chapter 6

Australian Water Dragons

Australian water dragons, sometimes called brown water dragons, are not as frequently seen in the pet trade as their green cousins. Because Australia does not export its wildlife, all Australian water dragons are captive bred. This means they cost more than green water dragons, but it also means that they are not usually carrying parasites or stressed from trying to adapt to captivity. On the whole, they are hardy, parasite resistant, and not shy of people—all traits that make them good pets.

Range

There are two subspecies of Australian water dragon, *Physignathus leseurii leseurii* and *P. l. howitti*. *P. lesueurii lesueurii* is found in New South Wales and Queensland. In New South Wales you'll find this subspecies in the central southern area of Albury and Wagga Wagga. It also lives north and northeast of the areas near Forbes, Dubbo, and Tamworth, and inhabits areas along the coast from about the Shoalhaven River to Queensland. In Queensland, this subspecies lives in a 100-150 mile (about 160-241 km) wide zone from Princess Charlotte Bay in the north to the border of New South Wales. This lizard goes by the name eastern water dragon in Australia.

The second subspecies is sometimes considered a full species, *P. howitti*. It is found in Victoria in Gippsland, in sections of the Australian Alps, and also in the area near Canberra and the Cullarin Range to the west of Sydney. Both subspecies are found in the Shoalhaven River area (e.g., Kangaroo Valley) (AHS, 1976). This river system is near Nowra, about 80 miles (about 129 km) southwest of Sydney.

Australian water dragons are not found in the moist tropical northern part of Australia, like Cape York or Arnhemland. They are also currently not found in New Guinea. However, until recently New Guinea was included in the range of the Australian water dragon. It is more likely that another lizard, such as *Hypsilurus* or *Hydrosaurus* was misidentified as a water dragon (De Rooij, 1915; Watkins-Colwell and Johnston, 1999). In addition, the animal on which this incorrect range information was based was purchased in 1871 from a dealer, which makes the true origin of the animal even more doubtful.

Australian water dragons range over most of Australia's east coast, except for the northernmost part.

In theory, this species needs a sufficiently long winter period for reproduction, probably because it occurs in more temperate than tropical climates. Furthermore, its range is limited by a need to be near bodies of water and a need for a sufficiently long summer period so that reproduction can take place before the fall weather arrives.

Habitat

The Australian water dragon is much less picky about his habitat than the green water dragon. Although permanent bodies of water, like rivers and lakes, surrounded by trees and forests are preferred, this species is found in a variety of other habitats. Members of the Australian Herpetological Society (AHS, 1976) even found this species in very polluted rivers frolicking between the floating garbage.

These lizards are also found in brackish water or on rocks at the seacoast, where they enter tidal zones in search of food (MacKay, 1959). Hoser (1989) wrote that these water dragons prefer to live in habits in which the tropical weed *Lantana camara* (or *Verbena*) grows. This weed gives excellent shelter between its branches and green leaves. It grows as a tall shrub and has pretty yellow and red flowers. This plant also grows many places in Florida. The Australian water dragon can also live around ponds and has been establishing territories in big cities like Sydney and Brisbane, where they are abundant in parks and gardens.

Climate

High temperatures of well above 100°F (about 38°C) occur everywhere in the habitat range of the Australian water dragon. However, during this extreme weather, these animals will hide in underground burrows or stay in the water. If you plan to keep these lizards outdoors in places where temperatures above 100°F (about 38°C) may occur, you need to provide them with cool underground shelters or with deep ponds. My experience with keeping these animals in captivity is that they do not like air temperatures above 95°F (about 35°C) and will seek cool shelter; temperatures over 100°F (about 38°C) may be lethal to them.

From the climate table, you can conclude that these water dragons are exposed to a rainy season in summer and a dry season in winter in the northern part of their range only, while in the southern part this is no longer the case. In Sydney, February to July gets the most rainfall, while in Canberra the precipitation is almost equally spread out over the year. Breeding seems to be triggered only by a sufficiently long cool period in winter. The lethal lower temperature was found to be 32°F (0°C); I have been surprised to find live Australian

Habitat Climate for the Coldest (July) and Warmest (January) Months of the Year

JANUARY

	AD Min	AD Max	HR	LR	%RH (9 am- 3 pm)	AMP
Townsville	76°F (26.1°C)	87°F (30.6°C)	104°F (40°C)	66°F (18.9°C)	73%-70%	10.9 inches (27.7 cm)
Brisbane	69°F (20.6°C	85°F (29.4°C)	110°F (43.3°C)	59°F (15°C)	66%-59%	6.4 inches (16.2 cm)
Sydney	65°F (18.3°C)	78°F (25.6°C)	114°F (45.6°C)	51°F (10.6°C)	68%-64%	3.5 inches (8.9 cm)
Bourke	70°F (21.1°C)	99°F (37.2°C)	125°F (51.7°C)	48°F (8.9°C)	42%-23%	1.4 inches (3.6 cm)
Canberra	55°F (12.8°C)	82°F (27.8°C)	109°F (42.8°C)	38°F (3.3°C)	56%-35%	1.9 inches (4.8 cm)

JULY

	AD Min	AD Max	HR	LR	%RH (9 am- 3 pm)	AMP
Townsville	59°F (15°C)	75°F (23.9°C)	85°F (29.4°C)	42°F (5.5°C)	64%-58%	0.6 inches (1.5 cm)
Brisbane	49°F (9.4°C)	68°F (20°C)	83°F (28.3°C)	36°F (2,2°C)	72%-51%	2.2 inches (5.6 cm)
Sydney	46°F (7.8°C)	60°F (15.6°C)	78°F (25.6°C)	36°F (2.2°C)	76%-60%	4.6 inches (11.7 cm)
Bourke	40°F (4.4°C)	65°F (18.3°C)	84°F (28.9°C)	26°F (-3.3°C)	74%-48%	0.9 inches (2.3 cm)
Canberra	33°F (0.6°C)	52°F (11.1°C)	65°F (18.3°C)	14°F (-10°C)	85% -63%	1.8 inches (4.6 cm)

Key: AD=average daily temperature; HR=highest recorded temperature; LR=lowest recorded temperature; RH=relative humidity; AMP=average monthly precipitation.

In the table, Townsville is at the north end of the range, Brisbane is in the middle, and Sydney is in the southern end of the range of *P. l. lesueurii.* Bourke is close to the most western point of the range of this subspecies. Canberra is near the most western point of the range of *P. l. howitii.* All these places have a period of an average daily maximum of at least 75°F (23.9°C), which is for five months or more. The water dragons are not found in Bourke, but close to it, so that you can see that within the range of *P. l. lesueurii* night frosts can occur. Within the range of *P. l. howitii* night frosts are quite normal in winter.

Although they are sometimes called brown water dragons, Australian water dragons, especially males, can be quite colorful.

water dragons in water below a thin layer of ice caused by an early and unexpected night frost.

It has also been noticed that these water dragons tolerate a wide range of relative air humidity levels. In winter, here in Alabama, I see them out and active with overcast weather and temperatures around 60°F (15.6°C). But when the sun shines, several come out to bask at air temperatures as low as 50°-54°F (10°-12.2°C). During sunny days, they may even be out basking at lower temperatures. On cooler days, this species and the crag lizards (*Cordylus melanotus subviridis*) that are also from the southern hemisphere are the only two species that emerge from their hiding places.

Description

When I saw these animals for the first time in a large outdoor enclosure at the Auckland Zoo in New Zealand, I was impressed by their beauty and elegance. The males had crests on their necks, their bodies were large and strong, and their heads were relatively big. The Australian water dragon, as a rule, grows a bit bigger and stronger than the green water dragon. Although the average total length of this species is between 2-2.5 feet (0.6-0.8m), there have been specimens that reached 3 feet (0.9 m) and over. In 1970, there was even a 4-foot long (1.2 m) specimen caught in Bundaberg, Queensland. The tail length was about 2.5 times the SVL.

Body

An adult Australian water dragon can weigh 1-1.5 lbs (0.5-0.7 kg), but specimens of over 2 lbs (0.9 kg) are found as well. The body and tail are slightly flattened in a vertical direction. The crest on the neck consists of long spiny scales, and the crest on the back has smaller spiny scales. The scales on top of the head are small and keeled. The occipital and temporal scales at the side of the head are larger, different in size, and often tubercular. The subocular scales do not form a ridge like in the green water dragon. There is a longitudinal line of enlarged scales at the sides of the chin. The lateral and dorsal scales are small and keeled, and between them are transversal lines of conical scales at the sides, hind legs, and tail root. The ventral and subcaudal scales are larger than the lateral scales and overlap each other. According to Bustard (1970), *P. l. howitii* has fewer spiny scales than *P. l. lesueurii*.

Coloration

The basic coloration of the Australian water dragon is gray, brown, and beige in all kinds of nuances. These colors are meant to let the animal blend in better with things in his habitat like tree trunks, boulders, and earth. Adult males have a more striking black and white coloration than females, especially the black stripe behind their eyes and the black bands on the back. Also, males have more striking white areas around their lips. In females, these stripes and bands are dark gray, and light gray on the lips. On the sides of the body, the lighter colored conical scales form light transversal bands. The throat and belly of the males of *P.l.lesueurii* is mostly red, but can also be yellow, as is the case in some regions of Queensland. The belly of females is often beige, but can also be pinkish and even red, as is the case in Sydney (Hardy and Hardy, 1977).

Male Australian water dragons have larger nuchal crests than the females.

The red coloration of the belly begins mostly when the young animals reach a total length of about 1 foot (30.5 cm). This is a good way to distinguish males from females, but it's not foolproof since some females, especially those from the Sydney area, can have red or pink colored bellies as well. A more accurate way to tell male from female is that the male has a larger head, larger crest, and has more intense white and black colors on the sides of the head. In females, the heads are smaller, crests are less high, and colors are duller.

The southern subspecies *P. l. howitii* has darker colors overall, perhaps because this allows them to thermoregulate better in a cooler climate. The black stripe behind the eye is unclear and often absent. The throat can have blue, orange, red, green, or yellow coloration.

Diet

The Australian water dragon is omnivorous and is very opportunistic regarding food. In mangrove forests, it will even hunt the crabs that are found there. Water dragons living on the coastline will enter the tidal zones and hunt for crabs or eat some species of sea grasses (MacKay, 1959; Ehmann, 1992). In the wild, the following items are also eaten: large insects (including cicadas, water beetles, and water striders), small lizards, frogs, tadpoles, mice, crayfish, fish, snails, and even carrion. They hunt both on land and in the water. For plant material, they eat flowers and fruits. Seeds of asparagus fern (*Asparagus retrofractus*) and other plants have been found in the feces of this species (Clifford and Hamley, 1982; Hardy and Hardy, 1977). So, just as birds do, Australian water dragons can spread plants in nature.

In captivity, Australian water dragons have eaten eastern water skinks (*Eulamprus quoyii*), slugs and water snails, ants, centipedes, maybeetles (*Melolontha*), fruits (apples, bananas, figs, strawberries, cherries, tomatoes, and grapes), yogurt, peanuts, meat (heart and liver of chickens and cows), cat food, and even small birds (Klingelhoeffer, 1957). Radek (1963) mentions that besides maybeetles, mealworms, and fruit, they even eat boiled eggs.

At my breeding facility, Australian water dragons live in large enclosures under semi-wild conditions. Here, just as is in the case of green water dragons, they do not accept vegetarian food. The feeding dish, present in all terrariums, is always filled with feeder insects. The continuous presence of insects may be a reason why fruits or flowers are not eaten; hibiscus flowers in the terrariums are never touched and neither are the ripe pineapple fruits. However, the insects are renewed daily in summertime and every second day during the cooler months of

Not So Different

Both species of water dragon require the same food and feeding methods. Like the green water dragon, the Australian water dragon rarely eats vegetation in captivity, although it does so in nature. See Chapter 3 for complete feeding information.

April, September, and October. In March, you occasionally feed according to the weather. Feed according to the climate and activity level of your dragons.

New feeder insects have usually eaten fruits or leaves, but a piece of carrot is added to the feeding dish so that the insects that are not eaten right away will be able to get carotene. The variety in the food sources comes mainly from the variety of food that the insects themselves are eating, which is very important. This works well, apparently, because these animals grow to be at least 10 years old and reproduce every year, and most of their eggs hatch and the babies grow fast.

At my facility, we used the superworm (*Zoophobas morio*) as the primary food source for the dragons from 1994 to 1999. This one feeder made up about 95 percent of the diet. Since 1999, the main food source has been the six-spotted cockroach of the genus *Eublaberus*. Occasionally, other food sources were insects and earthworms caught in these outdoor enclosures. However, frogs, salamanders, and lizards that lived in those same terrariums were not touched. Fire-bellied newts (*Cynops pyrrhogaster*), Chinese gliding frogs (*Polypedates dennysi*) and day geckos (*Phelsuma madagascariensis*) also lived with them in some terrariums. In other terrariums, local herps like treefrogs of the genus *Hyla*, anoles (*Anolis carolinensis*), or broad-headed skinks (*Eumeces laticeps*) entered regularly but were not chased either.

In the terrarium, Australian water dragons rarely eat plant matter.

Reproduction

Australian water dragons need a hibernation period for breeding. In central Alabama, where I live, they breed readily when kept in outdoors terraria, as I described earlier. In this area, you have a period of over six months with an average daily maximum temperature of 73°F (about 23°C) or higher from the middle of April to the third week of October. In Sydney, this period of an average daily maximum of 73°F (about 23°C) and higher is from the beginning of November to the beginning of April and is about a week shorter. I know from breeding these animals that the weather during the breeding season, which is during summer, is more important than the weather during the hibernation period.

Winters in central Alabama are colder than in Sydney. Therefore, my outdoor terrariums are dug into the ground and covered with plastic in winter. The plastic keeps the terrariums frost-free. Pineapple plants are used as indicator plants. When they survive, conditions are okay. The plastic filters the UVB out, but because Australian water dragons do not eat in winter, they also do not grow. In other words, metabolism is low during this time, so UVB is not needed because food is not being digested. In this way, conditions are very similar to those in and around Sydney. The transparent plastic is removed during warmer frost-free spells in winter. In central Alabama, it can be in the 70s (about 21 to 26°C) during in winter, and with sunlight it may get too warm inside the terrariums. By removing and covering the terrariums with plastic sheeting, you have a simple and cheap way to regulate the microclimate inside.

Australian water dragons breed more reliably when house outdoors rather than indoors.

Indoor Hibernation

If you live in an area where you cannot keep the Australian water dragons outdoors, but still want to breed them, then you will need to hibernate them indoors.

In the middle of September, you will have to start gradually reducing the temperature and photoperiod in the enclosure. While creating the shorter periods of light is as simple as adjusting a timer, for the lower temperatures in a heated room, you will need to change lightbulbs in the terrarium to a lower wattage or buy a dimmer. I believe that working with a dimmer is the easiest way. You can reduce the temperature a bit lower every week. Having a thermostat will also be helpful. The target temperature for hibernation is 50-55°F (10-12.8°C). If the room, where you have the terrarium is too warm all winter, then you must have another winter terrarium in a cooler room, enclosed porch, or basement.

While certain lizards will stay in their hibernation burrow for up to six months in a row, Australian water dragons emerge from time to time on warmer sunny winter days. Some such days, the temperatures in the enclosures reach the upper 70s (25-26°C). Even on these warm days when the lizards would come out, they do not eat. Therefore, it is probably best to give indoor hibernating animals the opportunity be active occasionally. It does not need to be a regular schedule; at my facility, the lizards may experience 10 days in a row with no basking opportunities, and then three days in a row with nice warm sunny winter weather.

By Februay, you must gradually start giving more light and warmer temperatures but no food yet. My Australian water dragons do not eat for at least five months, and they do not get skinny. Increase the photoperiod and temperatures gradually so that normal keeping conditions are established sometime between the middle and the end of March. In the outdoor enclosures here, the Australian water dragons start eating around the first of April, and inside they should start eating around then or a little earlier. Most people that try to breed this species indoors fail, but most people hibernate them for a too short time or not at all. I believe that a long hibernation stimulates breeding.

Australian water dragons breed when their hibernation period is over. It is hard to pinpoint the specific time that they emerge, because some animals would occasionally come out to bask during the winter period, although this tends to happen more frequently toward springtime. When Australian water dragons emerge during winter, they do not eat, and you should not encourage them to so either, because an extended cold season afterwards might kill them if they have undigested food in their intestines.

It is not always easy to tell what the exact period is between copulation and egg deposition. I have seen copulations at the end of March, and in April, May, and June. Female Australian water dragoons can store sperm for a short time. If the male is separated from the female before she lays her first clutch of eggs, a second clutch may still also produce fertile eggs. But if the male is not reintroduced after that, the female will produce infertile eggs the following year (Harlow and Harlow, 1977). But during most years, I found the Australian water dragon's first eggs between April 25th and 30th. As the first copulations I observed were at the end of March, I estimate that there are about four weeks between copulation and egg deposition.

Females always lay their eggs between 4 pm and 7 pm. The type of place they generally choose for egg deposition is an open piece of soil in a sunny spot. The soil can be sandy or just black garden soil. These females seem to have a slight preference for black garden soil, but will also readily choose sand to lay their eggs in. Later in the afternoon, when they actually lay their eggs, the sun is no longer shining on their chosen spot. In all my years of breeding, I never saw a female lay her eggs at another time of day. Also, I never saw a female making a nest in direct sunlight.

At 80°F (about 27°C) the incubation period is 68 to 74 days, and only males are born. At an incubation temperature of 82°-88°F (about 28-31°C) the incubation period is shorter, 56 to 60 days, and only females hatch. According to Harlow (1993, 1996), females will also hatch when the incubation temperature is 77°F (25°C) or lower.

Temperature-Dependent Sex Determination

Many lizard species have their sex determined not by genetics, but by the incubation temperature. This is called temperature-dependent sex determination (TDSD; sometimes TSD). With Australian water dragons, you see that males are produced at 80°F (about 27°C), while at higher and lower temperatures females are produced. If you researched only temperatures from 79°-85°F (about 26°-29°C), which is the most used incubation temperature, you would have concluded that males hatch at lower temperatures and females at higher temperatures in this species. But, as you know now, males are in the midrange.

During the late 1970s and early 1980s, I had similar experiences while breeding *Laudakia stellio* and *Laudakia caucasia*. At that time I was unaware that I was discovering an interesting, but still unknown phenomenon. The term TDSD had not yet been coined. I found it puzzling that all of the *Laudakia caucasia* babies I was hatching at 82.4°F (28°C) were males. The fact that when I lowered the incubation temperature to 79°F (26°C) or raised it to 88°F (31°C) females were produced was equally puzzling. When I mentioned these findings to other breeders or researchers, most of them simply smiled at me. "Bert, haven't you ever heard of x and y chromosomes?" However, two researchers, Carl Gans and Kraig Adler, found these notes very interesting. Also, from my background in physics, I knew that when you see a phenomenon, you should try to explain it, even if it seems a very odd one. It is now known with certainty that TDSD is a very real phenomenon and one that must be reckoned with by reptile breeders.

The biggest problem in validating TDSD in species is that, in most cases, you cannot sex the animals in the first half-year or year of life. By the time you can sex them, they are often sold, died, or were mixed with other animals. Also, no one looked out for this phenomenon in the years before 1970, so that it would only have been discovered by accident.

Some Observations

Since I started breeding this species in 1992 and until the fall of 2004, I have bred a total of 17,469 babies. Since I keep daily hatching notes, I have been able to split these numbers up by the month and year they were born. The earliest hatching date was June 17th and the

How Many Eggs?

When I was breeding in 2004, I counted the number of eggs per clutch for 166 nests. The number of eggs per clutch ranged from 3 to 14. Here are the exact results: There were 6 nests with 3 eggs; 10 nests with 4 eggs; 19 had 5 eggs; 22 had 6 eggs; 30 had 7 eggs; 29 had 8 eggs; 26 had 9 eggs; 11 had 10 eggs; 8 had 11 eggs; 3 had 12 eggs; one had 13 and one had 14 eggs. So you see that most of the nests (94% of the cases) contained 4 to 11 eggs. With this information, I could calculate the average number of eggs per nest and found it to be 7.36.

Female Australian water dragons generally lay seven or eight eggs in a clutch, but the number varies.

latest was October 6th. The number of babies hatched over this entire period per month are as follows: in June 147 babies were born, in July 6275, in August 9201, in September 1845, and in October only 1. If you make a diagram from this information, you can see that the beginning of August would be at the top of the chart. In most years, the first babies start hatching around the first of July and the last babies would hatch in the middle of September.

In 1995, I decided to perform a test. I wanted to incubate 200 eggs the natural way and see what happened. For that purpose, I measured the depth at which I found the eggs and moved them to a sandy place that I surrounded with a ring of vertically standing sheet metal to prevent any hatchlings from escaping. I dug them in just as deep as I originally found them, and put an accurate lab thermometer at the depth of the eggs. The incubation took place in June and July. The lowest temperature of 60°F (16°C) occurred very early one June morning. Throughout the rest of June, the lowest recorded early morning temperatures ranged from 64°-74°F (18°-23°C), while the highest afternoon temperatures ranged from 77°-89°F (25°-32°C). In July, the lowest early morning temperatures ranged from 71°F to 79°F (22°-26°C), while the highest afternoon temperatures ranged from 81°-92°F (27°-33°C). Temperatures from 90°-92°F (32°-33°C) were only noted for a short time on warm days and had no negative effect on the hatchlings. If, however, Australian water dragon eggs were incubated at a steady 90°-92°F (32°-33°C), deformations would be abundant.

To my surprise, all 200 eggs hatched under these conditions. At the same time, I stumbled onto a new phenomenon, because I discovered that all 200 babies hatched between 7 am and 9 am. Tentatively, I will baptize this phenomenon PHT (preferred hatching time). It must be expected that, as in nature, all babies of this species will hatch during early morning. During evolution, all babies that would hatch at night would be easy targets for predators, while others that would hatch around noon or in the afternoon would get killed when emerging to the surface on top of the hot sand. Early morning seems to be the perfect and safest time of the day for eggs to hatch in this species (Langerwerf, 1998)

Rearing Baby Australian Water Dragons

Rearing these babies is very easy. This species is not only hardy, but also quite social, so that many Australian water dragon babies can be kept together, a feature that is rare among agamid lizards. The terrarium you place them in can be made to feel larger by using twigs, branches, cardboard boxes, etc., which create various niches and spaces of all kinds that increase available surfaces for the babies to use. The best water bowls you can use for baby water dragons are paint roller trays, provided the terrarium is large enough. These trays have an angled bottom, which allows them to go in and out of the water easily. These trays are always placed in a shaded area, because the summer sun may make the water dangerously hot. The babies also use the space underneath these dishes as hiding place, because the water above keeps the temperature under the tray rather constant and cooler in summer. Therefore, you need to watch out when you do the daily cleaning. When emptying the dirty water, you may not see a baby that was under the dirt beneath the tray. Also, if you put the empty tray back and refill it, you may kill an animal with the increasing pressure of the heavy tray on top of it.

Hatchling Australian water dragons will grow rapidly during their first year of life.

When the babies are newly hatched, begin feeding them fruit flies, termites, and small crickets. You can sprinkle a lot of small termites into the terrarium, so that even the weaker babies get a chance to start taking food. When you only give just enough, the strong water dragon babies will devour most of the food before weaker ones get a chance to eat. The termites that are not eaten will nest in cardboard boxes inside the terrarium and can be eaten later on when these boxes are overturned. When feeding fruit flies, the solution is simple as well. Weeks before the babies are hatched, you can put boxes filled with overripe fruit in the terrarium. As soon as the babies are put in there, they will concentrate around these boxes to catch the fruit flies. For indoor housing, you can purchase colonies of flightless fruit flies from online herp supply stores, reptile expos, and some pet stores.

Safety Tip

Although termites are an excellent food for hatchling water dragons, you should probably not use them if you are keeping the lizards indoors. Escaped termites in the home can be disastrous.

When the babies grow, you can feed them more crickets and small superworms. Put the superworms in a feeder dish. If you are housing the babies outside, the dish should have a mesh bottom or other method of preventing it from filling with water during the rain. Quite often, some babies grow faster than others. The few water dragons that lag behind should be taken out and put in another terrarium. This must be done at the right time, and not when the smaller babies are too weak to be able to care for themselves. It's best to take out the largest ones first, so that the others have a better chance to grow.

Because babies that hatch out of an egg are free of many parasites like worms, protozoa, etc. (but not all bacteria or viruses), you can put them in terraria that have been empty for several months. The longer time that is, the better. The simplest way to deal with parasites is by staying ahead of them and keeping the babies free of them. By the time the first night frosts come and the babies start hiding underground, they must be strong animals at least 10-12 inches (25-31 cm) in total length. These will easily survive five months of winter in hibernation.

If you are trying to establish and maintain a breeding colony, always keep a number of hatchlings to reintroduce into your colony yearly. My facility has about 200 adult breeders. Given that the dragons live on average 10 to 15 years, I need to add at least 15 new animals every spring to maintain such a colony. This is 7.5 percent, which is a good number of hatchlings retained to keep the colony running.

Chapter 7

Similar Species

Agamidae is one of the largest families of lizards, and a number of species occur in the same habitat as water dragons or in habitat that is very similar. Some of these lizards show up in pet stores and at reptile expos, and some are even bred in captivity. This chapter will discuss some of these interesting lizards and their care—which you will find is not too dissimilar to that of the more common water dragons.

The sailfin lizards are the largest members of the family Agamidae and among the most visually impressive. *H. amboinensis* is shown.

Sailfin Dragons

One group of agamids that is occasionally imported and captive bred is the sailfin dragons. These lizards are placed in the genus *Hydrosaurus*. Imported sailfins are often stressed out and fail to adapt to captivity. If you want to keep these lizards, you are strongly encouraged to seek out captive-bred hatchlings or juveniles.

Hydrosaurus are the largest of all agamid lizards. They were first described as *Lophura* by Gray in 1827. A year later, in 1828, they were named *Hydrosaurus* by Kaup. Although several things still remain unclear regarding their taxonomy, these are the four species that are currently known: *H. amboinensis*, *H. microlophus*, *H. pustulatus*, and *H. weberi*. These impressive lizards are found on the islands of the Philippines, Indonesia, the Moluccas, and on New Guinea and a few others.

The taxonomy of the genus *Hydrosaurus* is poorly understood. To date, it is still unclear which of the above mentioned four species are true species and which are subspecies or varieties. It's also possible that the current species could be split into more species. There is no clear, straightforward key for this genus. Here are some reasons that may have caused the lack of knowledge about the taxonomy of the genus:

- The origin of the animal is often unclear because for centuries these animals were used as food or pets and were shipped to various market places.
- Within the known species, there is a high amount of variation in scalation and color. Also, the differences between young and old, or between male and female, are great, so that many features cannot be used to tell a species apart.
- The bureaucracy of the Philippines makes extensive research by herpetologists on the various islands very difficult.
- Most animals used for taxonomy purposes are preserved ones, so that colors have faded and, therefore, often only scalation is used to try to make a key of the species.

For captive propagation, this poor understanding of the species' taxonomy has some negative impact. First, it is impossible to be sure about the proper name of the species that

Salfin Dragon Species Natural Ranges

Species	Range
H. amboinensis	Ambon, Ceram, and New Guinea.
H. microlophus	Sulawesi
H. pustulatus	Philippines (except Palawan and the Sulu archipelago)
H. weberi	Halmahera and Ternate

is purchased, especially if the animals are wild caught and have gone through the hands of a number of dealers, exporters, or importers. For now, knowing the origin of the animal is the best way to determine which species you are getting. However, when animals have been collected on various islands in various countries, and then all come together at the hands of importers, it may no longer be possible to know the origin of these animals for sure. As a result, it's possible that you get animals from two different species, which is likely to make breeding impossible. Also, if you look at the climate in which they live, you see that the wet season is not the same in every range and can even be the opposite. So you can get animals from different climates, which makes it hard to create a wet season that suits all of the animals you have purchased. When purchasing sailfin dragons, therefore, you need to try to find the most similar looking animals that are available from a certain group, because that increases the odds that you have purchased animals that belong together on a species or subspecies level.

Description

Sailfin dragons can reach a total length of nearly 4 feet (up to 110 cm) and are, therefore, the largest agamid lizards. The most spectacular and also unique feature of these lizards is the large fin on the tail, which can be almost 5 inches (12.7 cm) high in some males. Also, there are crests on the neck and on the back. The top of the crest is decorated with a row of spiny scales. These spiny scales are triangular and very wide and high. Particularly in H. *pustulatus*, you can see a small crest on the tip of the snout. The toes of the hind leg possess strongly enlarged scales, which enables the animals to swim better. Males have larger femoral pores.

Range

Sailfin dragons live on many islands within the triangle formed by the island of Luzon in the north, the island of Sulawesi (Celebes) in the south, and the town of Wewak on the north coast of Papua New Guinea in the east. In New Guinea, they live only in the western and northwestern part, northwest of an imaginary line from Wanapiri on the south coast and Wewak on the north coast. On the Philippines, they live on most islands, but are lacking in the Palawan region at the far west of this nation.

Hydrosaurus weberi is found on the islands of Halmahera and Ternate, islands in the North Maluku province of Indonesia.

Habitat and Habits

These lizards live in a habitat similar to that of the green basilisk (*Basiliscus plumifrons*) in the New World, which is forest bordering rivers. Sailfins are always close to water bodies of any kind, and even brackish water is in their list of choice habitats. Mostly, they are found in the dense vegetation along lowland rivers. The babies can cross the rivers over the surface of the water by running in a bipedal way, similar to green basilisks. When threatened, the adults will also run over land in a bipedal way (Peters, 1974; Tayler, 1922; Gaulke, 1989).

They often rest on branches that hang over the water. They stick very much to their chosen place and in nature they can be found on the same branch in the morning or evening, and also the next week or next month. When they rest on a branch, they often dangle their legs at the sides of the branch. When it gets too hot during midday, they will retreat to more dense vegetation or go into the water. When they are on the forest floor, they keep their front limbs stretched and head high to overlook their surroundings.

In nature, just one adult male will be present in a group of sailfin dragons (Gaulke, 1989).

Male sailfin dragons develop larger crests than the females. This is the tail crest of a male *H. weberi*.

Sailfin dragons that are on the forest floor are very shy, and much shier than when they lay on branches that hang over the water. At any movement on the forest floor, they will bob their heads two to three times. When lizards of any kind enter their habitat, they will erect their crests, and make sideward movements with their tails. They will also open their mouths, and when caught, may bite very hard. For shedding they often choose the water basin (Visser, 1984). The water is also used for defecation.

Climate

The climate within the ranges of the species of *Hydrosaurus* has many things in common. The average daily minimum temperature is in the 70s (21-26°C) and the average daily maximum is in the 80s (27-32°C). The lowest recorded temperature in the range is 60°F (15.6°C), and the highest recorded is 101°F (38.3°C) Both of these temperatures were recorded in Manila.

Precipitation is high everywhere in their range. In most places, the wettest period falls around June, July, and August. But in Surigao (eastern Philippines), the wettest months are November, December, and January. Ambon is the wettest place; for three months in a row (May, June, and July) over 20 inches of precipitation occurs per month.

Terrarium

Sailfin dragons are, in general, very nervous lizards, and specifically wild-caught animals and babies often adapt poorly to captivity. They will need a lot of rest, which means no disturbance from movements seen through the glass sides of the terrarium. For this reason and to avoid nose bouncing, the glass needs to be covered for the first few weeks. Young animals are especially sensitive to stress, and they are much more difficult to settle in terraria than older animals (Krasula, 1988). Young animals often refuse to eat when the conditions they are kept in are not suitable. So, if baby *Hydrosaurus* do not feed, you need to address the way you are keeping them. You need to optimize the humidity and temperature, but most of

Quarantine Is Critical

The lizards discussed in this chapter are most often available only as wild-caught animals that will normally be carrying parasites and perhaps other pathogens. If you purchase one of these animals, it is critical to the health of your reptiles that you quarantine the new arrival in its own enclosure. During the quarantine, observe the lizard carefully for signs of health problems and take a stool sample to a vet to test for parasites.

all you need to provide them with a terrarium in which they feel safe and are not stressed.

After they adapt, the animals can still surprise you in the way they react in captivity. At the Zurich Zoo, there were two males, three females, and two babies kept in one terrarium without problems other than one male dominating—but not fighting with—the other male (Honegger, 1969). At the Rotterdam Zoo, three females could not be kept together because they did not tolerate each other's presence. It was even observed that a female attacked her own image in a mirror and tried to bite that image (Altmann, 1980). When threatened, even the normally dark brown H. pustulatus could change their body color rapidly to a bright greenish yellow coloration.

The terrarium for a small group of adult sailfin dragons needs to be large, especially if you want to breed with them (and captive breeding of any vulnerable or endangered species should be encouraged). Krasula (1988) bred them successfully in a terrarium 51 x 80 x 80 inches (1.3 x 2 x 2 m) in which one male and two females were kept. At the Rotterdam Zoo, they were kept and reproduced in a terrarium 126 x 80 x 91 inches (3.2 x 2 x 2.3 m), in which two males and two females were kept. In a terrarium for water dragons, you could do well with a rather small water bowl, but you need to have a large pond for the sailfin lizards. You will also need enough branches to offer climbing and shelters, so that the animals feel safe and comfortable.

The same terrarium setup and conditions that work for water dragons will work for sailfin dragons. They need plenty of sturdy climbing branches and a large—but easily cleaned—water area. Remember that these are shy and nervous lizards that require privacy.

Food

Hydrosaurus mainly feed on leaves and fruits. Research on the contents of their stomachs by Kopstein (1924, 1926) and Taylor (1922) shows that the adults eat mostly leaves, while the young ones prefer seeds. A preference for fruits of the *Ficus* species (figs) was noticed (Gaulke, 1989). They feed mainly during the morning and late afternoon, when the temperatures are a bit lower. They search the forest floor for edible plants, seeds, and fruits. Their preference seems to be yellow, orange, and red colors (Visser, 1984). In nature, it has not been observed that animal matter was taken as food. In the terrarium they feed on bananas, oranges, pears, apples, figs, leaves of willows, mulberries, lettuce, endive, dandelion, carrots, spinach, tomatoes, and salad greens. Also, they may eat tree bark (Lederer, 1931).

The sailfin dragons need a varied vegetarian diet. A female *H. weberi* is pictured eating an excellent meal.

In captivity, they may also chase and eat animals like locusts, mealworms, superworms, roaches, caterpillars, grubs, snails, butterflies, but also small rats, chicks, frogs, lizards, etc. It is doubtful if all this animal matter is good for these lizards, because in researching their eating habits in nature, they were never found to eat animal matter. In addition, Greg Watkins-Colwell (1993) writes that a *Hydrosaurus* died six weeks after eating a basilisk with a SVL of 4 inches (10.2 cm). Right after eating this lizard, which happened by accident, the *Hydrosaurus* refused all food.

In the Rotterdam Zoo, where they breed these lizards successfully, they are fed salad greens, carrots, tomatoes, bananas, oranges, apples, pears, pieces of chicken, meat, and a vitamin supplement six times per week. Once a week they are given crickets, locusts, mice or rats, and occasionally shrimp and small fish.

Hold the Lettuce

When feeding sailfins or other herbivorous lizards, you should avoid feeding iceberg and other lettuces. They are low in most nutrients. Instead, feed other more nutritious greens like dandelion leaves, collard greens, mustard greens, and parsley.

Reproduction

In nature, *Hydrosaurus* lay their eggs in sandy areas near rivers, just as green water dragons will. These nests are 8 to 12 inches (about 20-31 cm)

Sailfin dragons are being bred by hobbyists in small numbers. *H. amboinensis* and *H. weberi* are the most commonly bred species.

deep (Kopstein, 1924). Although they reproduce any time of the year, there is a peak in reproduction toward the end of the dry season (as seen in green water dragons in nature). This is between March and May for some areas of the Philippines (Gaulke, 1989).

There are several publications on the successful breeding of this species in captivity (Honegger, 1964; Krasula, 1988; Lederer, 1931; Nogge, 1983; Peters, 1974, Visser, 1984, 1988). Also, in captivity, they can reproduce any time of the year.

If females are gravid after a successful copulation, they tend to sleep in warmer places instead of on branches. If females are in optimal condition, they can lay up to 6 clutches of eggs per year. Each clutch contains 3 to 9 eggs, to a maximum of 11 eggs.

Freshly laid eggs are about 1.6 x 1 inch (4.1 x 2.5 cm) in size. After 70 days, these eggs have grown to a size of about 2.6 x 1.5 inches (6.6 x 3.8 cm). The eggs are incubated on moist peat or moist vermiculite. At an incubation temperature of 86°F (30°C), the babies hatch after 60 to 73 days, and at 82°F (28°C), the babies hatch after about 100 days. The babies have a total length of 6-10 inches (about 15-25 cm) at birth.

Mountain Horned Dragons

Mountain horned dragons, members of the genus *Acanthosaura*, are arboreal lizards that range across Southeast Asia, southern China, and parts of Indonesia. There are four member of the genus, and all of them occasionally show up in the pet trade. One, *A. capra*, is seen most frequently and captive bred in small numbers. When someone talks about mountain horned dragons, *A. capra* is usually the species they are referring to.

All four members of this genus have triangular heads and spiny crests (Gray, 1834). The care of each species is similar to water dragons. They require high humidity, at least 70 percent. These lizards are all insectivores and are not known to eat plant matter. Wild-caught individuals are generally dehydrated, stressed, and heavily parasitized. Your best chance of success will be to seek veterinary care as soon as possible after purchase or—better yet—to start with a captive-bred individual.

Acanthosaura armata

Acanthosaura armata ranges from southern Thailand to Singapore and is also found on the islands Penang, Tioman, and the Anamba Islands. It prefers the lower stem areas of trees in rain forests.

This species grows to a total length of up to 12 inches (30.5 cm). The high dorsal crest is formed with spiny scales; if these scales break, they will not grow

Acanthosaura armata is found in southern Thailand and some of the nearby islands.

back. The color is brownish to greenish. The males have two clearly visible hemipenal bulges at the tail root.

The terrarium must have a pool and several vertical tree stems. Avoid overheating; it's best to keep them at 72°-82°F (22°-28°C). Keep only one animal or one pair per terrarium. There are up to 21 eggs in a clutch. The incubation of the eggs can be done in moist vermiculate at 70°-77°F (21°-25°C) and will take 190 days. The babies are only half an inch long (1.27 cm) at birth. The babies prefer to eat slugs.

Acanthosaura capra

Acanthosaura capra lives in Cambodia, Laos, and Vietnam, where it is found in the tops of trees in the rainforest. In recent years, it has been imported into the US pet trade in substantial numbers, and some hobbyist breeders have had success reproducing this species.

The total length is 12 inches (30.5 cm). There is no spine on the back of the head, which is the way to tell this species apart from other species of this genus. The males have a large yellow dewlap that has greenish stripes. They have a high neck crest and a lower back crest. There is usually a green ring around the eye.

A. capra is the most common mountain horned dragon in the hobby and is captive bred in small numbers.

Along with the usual fare of insects, this species will eat small rodents, small lizards, and earthworms. The keeping temperatures for A. armata will suffice for this species as well.

Acanthosaura crucigera

Acanthosaura crucigera lives in southern Vietnam, Cambodia, Thailand, and Myanmar. They also live in northern Malaysia. The habitat is in the rainforest up to an altitude of 6000 feet (about 1.8 km).

The total length of this lizard is about 10 inches (about 25 cm). Females are almost an inch (2.5 cm) shorter than males. There are spiny scales above the eye, on the neck, and on the backs of these lizards. Males have a distinctive black coloration around and above the eye. They have overall beige colors with a reticulated pattern.

The terrarium must not be too warm; 70°-77 °F (21°-25°C) is the best temperature range. They need a big water bowl and abundant climbing branches. One clutch has 10 or more eggs. These eggs can be incubated in moist vermiculate at 77°F (25°C)and will hatch after about 200 days. They eat earthworms, grasshoppers, roaches, crickets, wax worms, pinky mice, and slugs.

The mountain horned dragons prefer slightly cooler temperatures than do water dragons. *A. cruicgera* is shown here.

Acanthosaura lepidogaster

Acanthosaura lepidogaster lives in southern China, Laos, Vietnam, Cambodia, North Thailand, Myanmar, and also on the island Hainan. It prefers sunny spots and roadsides in mountain forests. They are also often seen on the forest floor.

The total length of these lizards is about 11 inches (about 28 cm), but females are a bit smaller. There are spines above the eyes and on the back head, forming a crest. Their brownish coloration varies greatly according to the range in which they are found. There is often a dark spot behind the head on the neck.

The terrarium should be as in *A. crucigera*. Reproduction takes place after a cooling period of 6-8 weeks, during which the temperatures should be in the 50s (about 10-15°C). They eat earthworms, crickets, wax worms, superworms, and grasshoppers.

Gonocephalus

This is a group of spectacular Asian lizards, often called angle-headed dragons. There are now 16 species known in this genus (Kaup, 1825). They have no spines in the neck area and no protuberances on the snout. These lizards are rarely bred in captivity, so most of those offered for sale will be wild caught. Like the mountain horned dragons, they will be stressed, dehydrated, and parasitized; seek veterinary attention promptly. The care of these animals is very similar to that of green water dragons. The most common species are detailed here.

Gonocephalus bellii

Gonocephalus bellii lives on the Malay Peninsula and on the island of Pinang. It lives on thick tree stems near water. When disturbed, it flees upward into the trees. G. bellii is found at altitudes of up to 3200 feet (975 m).

The SVL of males is 5-6 inches (13-15 cm), and the SVL of females is 4-5 inches (10-13 cm). The total length is 20 inches (about 51 cm). The spines of the continuous back crest gradually get smaller toward the tail. The color of the males is quite variable, from blackish to dirty yellow or greenish. The color depends very much on the mood of the animal. The dewlap is bluish, sometimes with pink dots. The females have more brownish or reddish coloration, sometimes with yellow dots. Males have blue eyes and young ones and females have brown eyes.

At first, wild-caught animals need to adjust. They often do not feed well and must be kept in a quiet place. Once they are settled in the terrarium, they are no longer shy and feed well. Every two or three months, the female will lay three to five eggs. At 69°F (about 21°C), they need seven months to incubate and at 73°-77°F (23-25°C), they still need 136 days to incubate.

Gonocephalus borneensis

Gonocephalus borneensis lives in Borneo. It is found close to water on thick tree stems. This lizard's total length is about 17 inches (about 43 cm). Females are smaller. The crest,

Although several angle-headed dragons may have blue eyes, G. d. abbotti is often sold as the blue-eyed angle-head.

which is uninterrupted to the tail root is composed of lancet-shaped scales that are close together. The dewlap in both sexes is light colored, with dark interrupted stripes. The female is colored in the same way as females of G. bellii. When reproductively active, the female will lay four eggs about every three months.

Gonocephalus chamaeleontinus

Gonocephalus chamaeleontinus lives in Java, Sumatra, and Tioman in the lower tree stem areas of the rainforests.

Males grow to 13-18 inches (33 to 45.7 cm) long, but females are smaller. Their basic color is green on which you can see a reticulated design of light yellowish dots that are embedded with darker green. On their throat blue colors can be present. The tail has darker and lighter bands around it. There is a spiny crest on the back, head, and neck area. The crest scales are singly placed.

In the terrarium, they like to sit on horizontal branches. Keep only one animal or a pair per terrarium, as this species (and most of the others in the genus) is territorial. They breed all year and can lay one to seven eggs per clutch. When you incubate them in moist vermiculate at 82°F, they will hatch in 72 to 80 days. After two days the babies will eat small crickets; they are sexually mature at an age of three years. For food, they accept crickets, wax worms, earthworms, superworms, and pinky mice.

Gonocephalus doriae

This species has two subspecies: G. d. doriae lives on Borneo and G. d. abbotti lives on the peninsula formed by southern Thailand and Malaysia.

The total length is about 12 inches, of which 5 inches is the SVL. This species looks like G. chamaeleontinus, except that the crest scales in the neck are not singly placed, but overlap. Furthermore, they are lower and almost sickle shaped. The male of the nominate form is red with dark and light dots or greenish to olive colored. The juveniles and females are mostly monochrome green.

Insecure Lizards

Many of the lizards in this chapter are high-strung and often injure themselves by trying to flee through the enclosure glass. This is especially true of the sailfins and japaluras. Prevent this by giving these lizards spacious enclosures, plenty of cover, and hiding areas and also by covering the glass on three sides of the terrarium.

Gonocephalus grandis

Gonocephalus grandis lives on the Malay peninsula, and also on Tioman, Penang, Borneo, and Sumatra. It is always close to the water in the rainforest, where they can be found on stems, branches, and rocks.

The total length of males is up to 22 inches (55.9 cm), but females are a bit smaller. The males and females look very different. The female has a small neck crest and brown coloration, with transversal bands on the back. The male is green and has a large crest on the back of the head. The male has a blue color dotted with yellow spots on the lower sides.

The terrarium must have a large pond in it, with vertical and horizontal branches. Each terrarium should contain only one animal or one pair. Eggs that are left inside the terrarium incubate well at 66°-72°F and hatched after 75 to 90 days. The babies are about 4 inches (10.2 cm) at birth.

Gonocephalus kuhlii

Gonocephalus kuhlii is found on Java and Sumatra. It grows to a length of 9-11.5 inches (about 23-29 cm) of which 3-4 inches (about 8-10 cm) is the SVL. The babies have a total length of 3 inches (about 8 cm). They are similar to G. chamaeleontinus, but the neck crest is lower. In between the small dorsal scales are many large tubercular scales. The basic color is green. Females lay four eggs at a time.

Gonocephalus lacunosus

Gonocephalus lacunosus was only recently discovered in northern Sumatra, where the species lives in rainforests at over 3000 feet (about 914 m) altitude. There, it is found near brooks on thin trees.

The total length is 14-15 inches (36-38 cm). The SVL is 5-6 inches (13-15 cm). The male has a crest on the back, formed by lancet-shaped scales that lean slightly backward. The crest of the female is much smaller. There is also a crest on the neck. The males are dark green to dark gray, with enlarged yellow or green scales.

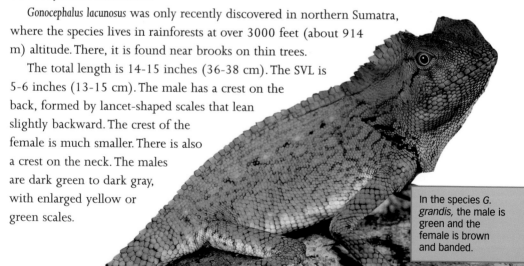

In the species G. grandis, the male is green and the female is brown and banded.

Gonocephalus liogaster

Gonocephalus liogaster lives in Malaysia, Borneo, Sumatra, and the Natuna archipelago. It prefers the stems of thick trees in the rainforest and are always near the water on trees or rocks.

The lizard may grow as long as 18-22 inches (about 46-59 cm). The females are smaller. They have a crest that runs from the neck to the tail root. This crest is larger in the males. The coloration is brownish, greenish, or reddish, and the tail has darker and lighter bands. In the terrarium, they will eat crickets, grasshoppers, wax worms, roaches, superworms, and mealworms.

They can lay three eggs, which hatch after 97 days when they are incubated at 68°-76°F (about 20°-24°C)

Head Like an Angle

The lizards in the genus *Gonocephalus* are often called angle-headed dragons or just angle-heads. The word *Gonocephalus* actually means "angular or square head." This refers to the bony crest that runs from over the eye to the nostril and which forms a sharp angle above each eye.

Hypsilurus

Hypsilurus looks much like the genus Gonocephalus (Peters 1876) and was actually considered part of Gonocephalus until recently. The two groups of lizards are very difficult to tell apart externally. These lizards are often called forest dragons and are found in Australia, New Guinea, Micronesia, and Melanesia.

Hypsilurus boydii

Hypsilurus boydii lives in northeast Queensland, Australia. It is found in rainforests and is always near rivers. The species lives on the lower stem areas of trees, but can also be seen on the forest floor. Because the species is endemic to Australia, they are essentially absent from the pet trade. If you encounter this animal for sale, you must be sure it is captive-bred from legal stock before purchasing.

Males may be up to 18 inches (about 46 cm) long, but females do not reach quite this length. The color of H. boydii is gray to red brown. Under the throat are spiny scales. The rear lower jaw area has enlarged scales of a whitish color. There is a large crest on the neck and also a crest on the back. The tail has dark bands.

Hypsilurus dilophus

Hypsilurus dilophus lives in New Guinea and some surrounding islands. It is found on tree branches near water in the rainforests.

The total length is nearly 2 feet (0.6 cm), but females are smaller. A crest of large spines is present on the head, the back, and on the first half of the tail. The basic color is dark brown to yellow green, on which you can see light colored, large tubercular scales that seem to form transversal lines. There are spiny scales on the chin, too. Males have wider tail roots, and also a red iris and a red ring around the eye. The normal clutch seems to be two eggs, which are laid in moist soil. In captivity, they eat grasshoppers, crickets, roaches, superworms, and pinky mice.

Hypsilurus godeffroyi

Hypsilurus godeffroyi lives on the Solomon and Caroline Islands and also in New Guinea, where it is found on stems and branches in the rain forest.

H. godeffroyi may be 24-28 inches (about 61-71 cm) long. A crest is formed of lancet-like triangular scales and runs continuously from the back of the head to the first third of the tail. These triangular scales sit on top of a skin fin. The dorsal scales are smaller than the ventral scales. Males and females have a dewlap. The males are gray green to gray brown, while the last part of the body and the start of the tail often have a mallow-like coloration. The dewlap has a beige to gray color, with yellow, orange, or black round dots on it. The females are green, with black spots on the sides. The belly is yellow to yellow-green.

Hypsilurus godeffroyi ranges across New Guinea, the Solomon Islands, and the Caroline Islands.

They eat insects and rarely other lizards, fruits, and plants. They lay two to three eggs that hatch after six to eight weeks.

Hypsilurus spinipes

Hypsilurus *spinipes* lives at an altitude of 160-3700 feet (48.8 to 1,123 m) in the rainforests of the Great Dividing Range at Australia's east coast, where it is found between Gympie in the north and Gosford in the south. Because it is restricted to Australia, it is almost never found in the international pet trade, but it is kept often by herp hobbyists living in that country.

Males have a home range of 3000-7000 sq feet (914-2134 sq m), in which they do not tolerate other males. Also females seem to protect their home range against intruders.

Their SVL is almost 4.5 inches (about 11 cm) and the tail length is about 9-10 inches (about 23-25 cm).

On the neck, there is a fin-like crest of skin with triangular comb scales. Similar scales run over the top of the back. The basic color is light brownish gray, with an irregular pattern on it. On top of the eye are several dark stripes that radiate away from the eye.

The air temperature at which they are active is between 60°-77°F (about 16°-25°C).

They lay two to seven eggs per clutch, which can be incubated at 63°-68°F (about 17-20°C) and will hatch after 74 days. After they hatch, the babies often play dead.

Japalura

The genus *Japalura* contains at least 20 species of mid-sized insectivorous lizards. They are normally called mountain lizards or japaluras by hobbyists. Their bodies are laterally compressed and their tails are long—up to twice the SVL. Coloration varies but is primarily composed of browns and greens. Japaluras are lizards of montane rainforests across Southeast Asia, Japan, China, and the Indo-Australian archipelago. Given their habitat, they require moderately high humidity and misting.

Japaluras are usually wild-caught and suffer from all the problems relating to that. The species are sometimes difficult to tell apart. Only one appears regularly in the US hobby, but it is possible others could be imported.

Confusing Japaluras

The japaluras are a large and confusing group of lizards. There are about 24 known species, many of which are very similar. It may be impossible to know just what species you have. Additionally, there is a real chance that there are more species than those recognized. Because of this, figuring out the proper care of a japalura you purchase can be tricky. Provide the conditions appropriate for *Japalura splendida* and observe your pet to see how its doing. If it always stays near the lights, it may need higher temperatures. If it stays in the water bowl, it probably needs higher humidity. By paying attention to your japalura's behavior, you should be able to figure out the conditions it needs.

Dragon Agama

The dragon agama, *Japalura splendida*, lives in southwestern China, where it has been found in the provinces of Hunan, Hubei, Guizhou, Yunnan, Sichuan, Gansu, and Henan. It usually is found in trees.

Chongqing, which is on the border of the provinces Sichuan and Guizhou, is in the middle of the range of this species. Here, winters are cool and have average minimum temperatures in January of 41°F (5°C) and the lowest recorded is 29°F (-1.7°C). Summers are long and hot, with July and August having average maxima in the mid 90s (about 32-37°C), with 111°F (44°C) as the highest temperature recorded. Summers are wetter (June has 7.1 inches (18 cm) of precipitation) than winters (January has 0.6 inches (1.5 cm)).

Their total length is 12 inches (30.5 cm), but females are a bit smaller. They have a crest on the neck and a small crest on the back. The basic coloration is green, with a wide yellow to green dorsolateral stripe that runs from the neck to the tail base. The top lip is almost white. The sides are darker.

The species of Japalura are difficult to identify, and it is unclear how many species are in the hobby. This is *J. flaviceps.*

Their terrarium must have abundant climbing branches. I have kept some outdoors in Alabama in terraria that I could cover in winter. They displayed about the same lifestyle as the local anoles, but could not climb smooth materials like anoles can. The winter was survived by a few but not by all.

Personal Experience In the spring of 2002, I obtained a small colony of dragon agamas, because from the literature I knew that nothing was yet known about the reproduction

The dragon agama is found in montane rainforests of China.

of this species. These animals are very inexpensive and thus not interesting to commercial breeders, so I only kept them for a year to research their reproduction.

On June 19, 2002, I saw one female laying eggs. After she was done, I collected the eggs for incubation and checked further nests. I found a total of three nests. They were not very deep, 2-3 inches (about 5-8 cm), and made in rather dry soil. The female had chosen the driest area of the terrarium to lay her eggs. This is probably because in China reproduction occurs during rainy season and a drier area is less likely to flood or become too wet than an area that is already wet.

One nest had seven eggs, while the other two nests had six eggs each. I measured one of the eggs from the recently laid clutch. This egg was six-sixteenths inches (15 mm) long and three-sixteenths inches (5 mm) wide.

Babies hatched on July 15th, July 16th, and July 17th from the nests that were laid before June 19th. I measured one baby and found it to have an SVL of 1.0 inch and a tail length of 1.8 in (2.5 and 4.6 cm). The total length, therefore, was 2.8 in (7.2 cm). On August 5th five babies hatched from the nest that was laid on June 19th. On August 9th another baby hatched from that nest. The incubation temperature was around 82°F (about

28°C) and the incubation period was thus 47 to 51 days. On August 19th a few more babies hatched from eggs that I found later. The babies fed on small termites, fruit flies, and small crickets. The adults ate superworms, earthworms, crickets, flies, and wax worms.

When you take into account about 50 days for incubation, you find that the eggs that hatched in mid July must have been deposited at some date at the end of May, while the eggs that hatched on August 19th must have been deposited at the end of June. This brings the egg deposition period to at least from the end of May to the end of June.

A dragon agama in the author's outdoor enclosure. These lizards bred successfully in this setup.

Striped Water Dragons

The striped water dragons are a small group of species placed in the genus *Lophognathus*. Except for *L. temporalis*, the Papuan water dragon, and *L. maculilabris* these lizards are confined to Australia and therefore unavailable. The Papuan water dragon turns up in the pet trade on rare occasions.

Description

Members of this genus have a very long tail, which is about three-quarters of the total length of the body. They also have a skin fold just behind their cheeks at the sides of their necks. In case of danger, the animal can enlarge this skin fold in order to give a larger appearance. There are also spiny scales on that skin fold. The appearance of this genus somewhat resembles that of the striped basilisk (*Basiliscus vittatus*) that lives in a similar habitat but belongs to an entirely different family Corytophanidae).

In this genus, the males possess wider cheeks and better developed femoral and pre-anal pores than the females. The males also have wider tail roots, so that it is relatively easy to tell the sexes apart in adult animals. In young animals, however, it is not possible to sex them by these features.

Habitat

Except for *L. longirostris*, these lizards live near bodies of water. They like to climb on plants or

trees near water so that, if they sense danger, they can jump down and seek shelter in the water. When the danger passes, they will climb up on the banks and look for a tree to climb again.

The lizards of this genus can live in quite high densities. Baehr (1976) could count 18 examples during a walk of less than a mile (1.5 kilometers). Their food consists of insects, spiders, small lizards, etc.

Since Australia closed its borders to the export of wildlife in the 1970s, you will only see *L. temporalis* from New Guinea on the market. This genus, as a whole, is also much harder to reproduce in captivity than the genus *Physignatus*.

The terrarium for these lizards needs to contain lots of branches and other climbing possibilities. Additionally, it can be similar to the terrarium for the lizards of the genus *Physignatus*. See Chapter 2 for housing information on water dragons, which can be adapted to *Lophognathus*.

Because it is the only species of *Lophognathus* found outside of *Australia, L.* temporalis is the only one that is seen in the pet trade.

Lophognathus maculilabris

L. maculilabris is a mysterious species from an island near Timor. They were described by Boulenger in 1883. Only two females were found. Their SVL is almost 4 inches (about 10 cm), and their tail length almost 12 inches (about 31 cm). The head and throat have strongly keeled scales; dorsal scales are strongly keeled as well. The ventral scales are strongly keeled and larger than the dorsal scales. The known females had no femoral or pre-anal pores. On the sides are black, white edged transverse stripes. Around the eyes, black lines radiate in a star-like pattern. The belly is whitish with dark points.

There is a chance this lizard could enter the pet trade. Indonesia does export its fauna, so this lizard could someday be collected and exported.

Lophognathus temporalis

L. temporalis is the most imported species of this genus and, therefore, the best known. They are sometimes sold as Australian water dragons. The species is found in northernmost Australia, except Cape York. The other half of their range is in southern New Guinea, where they live south of the east and west mountain ranges. The most eastern point of their range is Port Moresby in Papua New Guinea. They are also found on a few Indonesian islands between Timor and New Guinea: Kai, Babar, Tanimbar, and Damar.

The SVL is 4 to 4.4 inches (10-11 cm), while the tail is about two to four times as long as the SVL. According to Storr (1974), the tail can even be up to 4.6 times longer. On the neck and back, they have small crests, which are formed by enlarged spiny scales. These crests are clearly larger in the males. The dorsal scales are uniform and small, and the keels on them point in the direction of the crests. At the rear of the cheeks are some enlarged tubercular scales. The nostril is closer to the tip of the snout than to the eye, which is a good way to distinguish this species from the similarly sized *L. longirostris*. The gular scales are smooth, and the ventral scales are larger than the dorsal scales and are average to strongly keeled. The throat skin fold is clearly expressed.

They have one to three femoral pores and one to two pre-anal pores. The light-colored dorsolateral stripe is a sharp contrast to the gray to red-brown body coloration. This stripe runs to the tip of the snout, giving the lizards nice light lips, and continues to the area near the hind legs and tail base. The top of the stripe almost reaches the eardrum and the eye. In males, the stripe is much more clearly expressed than in females. The animals can change the coloration of the stripe rapidly from a suppressed coloration to a bright color. Between the eye and the eardrum, there is often a dark spot. The throat is whitish gray.

Blamires (1998) observed that males would bob their heads if he approached them, after which they would flee. When they were on a tree trunk, they would always flee to the back of that trunk so that they could not be seen (Blamires, 1999).

Female *Lophognathus gilberti*. This species is found in a variety of habitats across most of northern Australia.

This species lives in a typical water dragon environment consisting of marshes, brooks, lagoons, and other water bodies that are surrounded by trees and bushes. In Darwin, Australia, they are often seen in parks and gardens (Blamires, 1999).

The climate in which they live is as follows. In Port Moresby, the average daily minimum is 73°-76°F (23°-24°C) throughout the year. The lowest recorded temperature is 64°F (about 18°C). The average daily maximum varies from 82°-90°F (about 28°-32°C) throughout the year. August is the driest month with less then 1 inch (2.5 cm) of precipitation. The months June through November have less than 2 inches (5.1 cm) precipitation per month. January, February, and March have over 6 inches (15.2 cm) of precipitation per month and is the middle of the rainy season. During the dry season, the overall temperatures are a bit lower than during the wet season.

Name Change

Lophognathus was part of the genus *Physignathus* until 1980 (Moody, 1980) and, therefore, a summary of the species of this genus follows.

The name *Lophognathus* was first used by Gray in 1842. He later used the name *Lophognathus gilberti*. In 1885, Boulenger moved this genus to the genus *Physignathus,* until Moody suggested in 1980 that the genus again be named *Lophognathus*. Cogger et al. (1983) and Baverstock and Donnellan (1990) agreed with the opinion of Moody.

This species has been difficult to reproduce in the terrarium. Probably, a cycle of dry and wet seasons may stimulate reproduction in captivity. In nature, this species starts a phase of inactivity in the middle of the dry season, during which the body temperature is also reduced by means of thermoregulation (Christian et al., 1999; Greer, 1990; James and Shine, 1985). The metabolism is lower then. These lizards hide a lot during the dry season.

In Darwin, the reproductive season is connected to the rainy season, which is from September to February. But because you heat your terrarium, you tend to keep it drier in winter than in summer. When the temperature difference between the two spaces (the inside and the outside of the terrarium) is higher, so is the difference in water vapor pressure. As a result, water will flow out of the terrarium faster in the form of vapor during the winter season than during the summer season. Having this in mind, you may want to consider moving the wet season or breeding season for these lizards to the summer, when it is easier to keep terrariums moist enough. They lay two to six eggs per clutch.

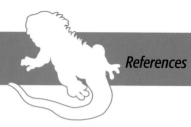

Antonini, O. 2004. "*Physignathus lesueurii* Gray 1831," *Reptil Mag.*, 16.

Australian Herpetological Society (AHS). 1976: "Observations on the eastern water dragon *Physignathus lesueurii* in the natural state and captivity," *Herpetofauna*, 8(2).

Baehr, M. 1976 "Beobachtungen zur bipeden Fortbewegung bei der australischen Agame *Physignathus longirostris* Boulenger," *Stuttgarter Beitrage zur Naturkunde Serie A Biologie*, 291: 1-7.

Baverstock, P. R. and S. C. Donnellan. 1990. "Molecular evolution in Australian dragons and skinks: progress report," *Memoirs of the Queensland Museum*, 29: 323-331.

Blamires, S. J. 1998. "Circumduction and head bobbing in the agamid lizard *Lophognathus temporalis*," *Herpetofauna*, 28 (1): 51-52.

Blamires, S. J. 1999. "Factors influencing the escape response of an arboreal agamid lizard of tropical Australia *Lophognatus temporalis* in an urban environment.," *Canadian Journal of Zoology,*, 77: 1998-2003.

Boulenger, G. A. 1883. "Remarks on the lizards of the genus *Lophognathus*," *Ann.Mag. Nat. Hist.*, 5(12): 225-226.

Boulenger, G. A. 1885. *Catalogue of the Lizards in the British Museum (Natural History)*. London: Vol. 1, 2nd Ed.

Bustard, R. 1970: *Australian Lizards*. Sydney, London: William Collins Ltd.

Christian, K. A., G. Bedford, B. Green, A. Griffiths, and N. Newgrain. 1999. "Physiological ecology of a tropical dragon *Lophognathus temporalis*," *Australian Journal of Ecology*, 24(2): 171-181.

Cogger, H. G., E. Cameron, and H. M. Cogger. 1983. *Zoological Catalogue of Australia (Amphibia and Reptilia)*. Canberra: Austr. Government Publ. Service.

Cogger, H. G. 2000. *Reptiles and Amphibians of Australia*. Chatswood, NSW: Reed Books, 6th Ed., and Ithaca, NY: Cornell Univ. Press.

DeBitter, H. M. 1986. "Bevruchte eieren van twee groene wateragamen, *Physignathus cocincinus*, dankzij spermaopslag?" *Lacerta*, 44(5), 74-76, 1986.

De Rooij. 1915. *The Reptiles of the Indo–Australian Archipelago.* Leiden: Brill Ltd, 66-137.

Clifford, H. T. and T. Hamley. 1982. "Seed dispersal by water dragons," *Queensland Naturalist,* 23(5) 6-49.

Dedekind, K and H. G. Petzold. 1982. "Zur Haltung und Zucht der hinterindischen Wasseragame *Physignathus cocincinus* Cuvier 1829 im Tierpark," *Berlin m Zoologischer Garten,* 52(1): 29 45.

Ehmann, H. 1992. *Encyclopedia of Australian Reptiles.* Australia: Angus and Robertson.

Er-Mi, Zhao and K. Adler.1993: *Herpetology of China.* Soc. Study Amph. Rept.

Floericke, K. 1912. *Kriechtiere u. Lurche fremder Länder Kosmos.* Stuttgart.

Friederich,U. and W.Volland. 1992. *Futtertierzucht Cultures of Feeder Animals.* Stuttgart: Ulmer Verlag.

Gaulke, M. 1989. "Einige Bemerkungen ueber die philippinische Segelechse *Hydrosaurus pustulatus* eschscholtz, 1829," *Herpetofauna,Weinstadt,* 11(62): 6 12.

Graham, G. M. and P. Strimple. 1998. "Green water dragons, jewels of the forest," *Reptiles,* May, 1998.

Greer, A. E. 1990. *The Biology and Evolution of Australian Frogs and Reptiles.* Sydney: Surrey Beatty and Sons.

Hardy, C. J. and C. M. Hardy. 1977. "Tail regeneration and other observations in a species of agamid lizards," *Australian Zoology,* 19(2): 141-148.

Harlow, P. 1993. "Life history attributes of an agamid lizard with temperature dependent sex," *Abstracts, Second World Congress of Herpetology,* Sydney.

Harlow, P. 1996. Personal Communication. University of Sydney.

Harlow, P. S. and F. M.Harlow. 1977. "Captive reproduction and longevity in the eastern water dragon *Physignathus lesueurii,*" Herpetofauna, 27(1): 14-19.

Henkel, F. W. and W. Schmidt. 1997. *Agamen im Terrarium.* Landbuch, Hannover.

Honegger, R. E. and C. R. Schmidt. 1964. "Herpetologisches aus dem Züricher Zoo. 1. beiträge zur Haltung und Zucht verschiedener Reptilien," *Aq. Und Terr. Zeitschrift.,* 17: 339-342.

Hoser, R. 1989. *Australian Reptiles and Frogs.* Sydney: Pierson and Co.

James, C. D. and R. Shine. 1985. 'The seasonal timing of reproduction: a tropic temperate comparison in Australian lizards," *Oecologia,* 67: 464-476.

Jauch, H. 1979: "Beobachtungen an asiatischen Wasseragamen *Physignathus cocincinus*," *Herpetofauna,Weinstadt*, 1(2): 15-17.

Kammerer. 1999. "Haltung und Nachzucht von *Physignathus cocincinus*," *Elaphe N.F.*, 7(1): 22-24.

Klingelhöffer, W. 1957. *Terrarienkunde*. Stuttgart: Alfred Kernen Verlag, Vol. 3.

Kopstein, P. F. 1924. "Tierbilder aus den Molukken.," *Natuurk.Tijdschrift. Ned. Indie* 84(2): 89-93.

Kopstein, P .F. 1926. "Reptilien von den Molukken und den benachbarten Inseln," *Zool. Mededel. Leiden*, 9: 79-81.

Krasula, K. 1988. "Haltung und Nachzucht der Segelechse *Hydrosaurus pustulatus*," *Herpetofauna, Weinstadt*, 10(53): 30-34.

Langerwerf, B. 1983. "Uber die Haltung und Zucht von agama caucasia eichwald 1831 sauria, agamidae salamandra," *Frankfurt/Main*.

Langerwerf, B. 1998. "Einfluss schwankender Temperaturen auf den Schlupf bei zwei Echsenarten," *Elaphe*, 6(3).

Langerwerf, B. 1999, 2000. "Die Australische Wasseragame, *Physignathus lesueurii*," *Reptilia*, Dec 1999/Jan 2000, 32-39.

Langerwerf, B. 2002/2003. "Neue Erkenntnisse über die Fortpflanzungsstrategie beim Argentinischen Riesenteju *T.merianae*," *Reptilia*, Dec 2002/Jan 2003.

Lederer, G. 1931. "Ein weiterer Beitrag zur Ethologie der Segelechse *Hydrosaurus amboinensis* schloss," *Zoologischer Garten*, 4: 277-279.

Macey, J. R., J. A.Schulte, A. Larson, N. B. Ananyeva, Y. Z. Wang, R. Pethiyagoda, N. Rastegar Pouyani, and T. J. Papenfuss. 2000. "Evaluating trans tetys migration: An example using acrodont lizard phylogenetics," *Systematic Biology*, 49(2): 233-256.

MacKay, R. D. 1959. "Reptiles of Lion Island," *NSW Australian Zoologist*, 12: 308-309.

Manthey, S and U. Manthey. 1999/2000, "Beobachtungen an *Physignathus cocincinus* in Thailand und Laos," *Reptilia*, Dec 1999/Jan 2000.

Manthey, U. and N. Schuster. 1992. *Agamen Herpetologischer Fachverlag Muenster*

Mercolli, C. and A. Yanosky. 1994. "The diet of adult *Tupinambis merianae* in the eastern Chaco of Argentina," *The Herpetological Journal*, 4(1): 15-19.

Miller, K, T. Wadding, and R. Meek. 2004. "Effect of husbandry manipulations on respiratory rates in captive bearded dragons *Pogona vitticeps*," *The Herpetological Bulletin*, 87, Spring.

Montague, P. D. 1914. "A report on the fauna of the Monte Bello Islands," *Proc. Zool. Soc.* London, 625-652.

Moody, S. M. 1980. "Phylogenetic and historical biographical relationship of the genera in the family Agamidae Reptilia: Lacertilia," *Ph.D.Thesis, Univ.of Michigan at Ann Arbor*.

Nietzke, G. 1980. *Die Terrarientiere*. Stuttgart: Ulmer Verlag, 151-152.

Nogge, G. 1983. "Jahresbericht 1982 der Aktiengesellschaft Zoologischer Garten Köln. – Kölner Zoo," 26(1): 13.

Pearce, E. A. and C. G.Smith, 1998. *World Weather Guide*. Fodor's series.

Radel, G. 1963. "De Wateragaam," *Lacerta*, 21(4), January 1963.

Schilliger, L. 2004. "Le sex ratio thermodependant, comment ca marche?," *Repil Mag*. 15.

Schliemann, D. 1968. "Die Haltung von cochinchina Wasseragamen *Physignathus cocincinus*," *Aqua Terra*, 5:81-83.

Smith, M. A. 1935. *Reptiles and Amphibians,Vol.II,The Fauna of British India, Including Ceylon and Burma*. London: Taylor & Francis.

Storr, G. M. 1974. "Agamid lizards of the genera *Caimanops, Physignathus* and *Diporiphora* in Western Australia and Northern Territory," *Records,Western Australian Museum*, 3(2): 121-146.

Taylor, E. H. 1963. "The lizards of Thailand," *Kans.Uni.Sci.Bull., Lawrence*, 44: 687-1077.

Tomey, W. A. 1985. "Grüner Baumdrache. *Physignathus cocincinus* aus dem nebelwald aquarium," *Bornheim*, 19(194): 425-427.

Ullrich, K. 1979. "Angaben zur zucht von Ph.cocincinus," *Herpetofauna*, 1(2): 17.

Visser, G. 1984. "Husbandry and reproduction of the sailtailed lizard, *Hydrosaurus amboinensis schlosser*, 1768 at Rotterdam Zoo," *Acta Zool.Path.Antverp.*, 78: 129-148.

Visser, G. 1988. "Verzorging en kweek van de ambonese zeilhagedis *Hydrosaurus amboinensis*," *Lacerta*, 46(4): 54-61.

Vogel, Z. 1969. "Die mini Saurier," *Aquarien Magazin*, 3(10): 406-408.

Watkins Colwell, G. J. and G. Johnston. 1999. "Does the water dragon, *Physignathus lesueurii* Gray, 1931 occur in New Guinea?," *Herpetological Review*, 30(2):73-74.

Werning, H. 1999/2000. "Wasseragamen" *Reptilia*, Dec 1999/Jan 2000, 16-21.

Werning, H. 2002. *Wasseragamen und Segelechsen*. Natur und Tier Verlag. Müenster, Germany.

Worrell, E. 1963. *Reptiles of Australia*. Sydney: Angus and Robertson.

Zhao, E. and K. Adler. 1993. *Herpetology of China*. Society for the Study of Amphibians and Reptiles.

Ziegler, T. 2002. "Die amphibien und Reptilien eines Tieflandfeuchtwald Shützgebietes in Vietnam." Natur und Tier Verlag. Müenster, Germany.

Zwart, P. 1977. "Ca:P versorgung bei reptilien und durch defizienten verursachte krankheiten," Lecture given in Vienna, 1977.

Zwart, P. 1980. "Nutrition and nutritional disturbances in reptiles," Paper presented at the International Herpetological Symposium, Oxford, 1980.

CLUBS AND SOCIETIES

Amphibian, Reptile & Insect Association
Liz Price
23 Windmill Rd
Irthlingsborough
Wellingborough NN9 5RJ
England

American Society of Ichthyologists and Herpetologists
Maureen Donnelly, Secretary
Grice Marine Laboratory
Florida International University
Biological Sciences
11200 SW 8th St.
Miami, FL 33199
Telephone: (305) 348-1235
E-mail: asih@fiu.edu
www.asih.org

International Herpetological Society
c/o Carol Friend
15 Barnett Lane
Wordsley
West Midlands
DY8 5PZ
United Kingdom

Society for the Study of Amphibians and Reptiles (SSAR)
Marion Preest, Secretary
The Claremont Colleges
925 N. Mills Ave.
Claremont, CA 91711
Telephone: 909-607-8014
E-mail: mpreest@jsd.claremont.edu
www.ssarherps.org

VETERINARY RESOURCES

Association of Reptile and Amphibian Veterinarians (ARAV)
P.O. Box 605
Chester Heights, PA 19017
Phone: 610-358-9530
Fax: 610-892-4813
E-mail: ARAVETS@aol.com
www.arav.org

RESCUE AND ADOPTION SERVICES

ASPCA
424 East 92nd Street
New York, NY 10128-6801
Phone: (212) 876-7700
E-mail: information@aspca.org
www.aspca.org

New England Amphibian and Reptile Rescue
www.nearr.com

Petfinder.com
www.petfinder.org

Reptile Rescue, Canada
http://www.reptilerescue.on.ca

RSPCA (UK)
Wilberforce Way
Southwater
Horsham, West Sussex RH13 9RS
Telephone: 0870 3335 999
www.rspca.org.uk

WEBSITES

Federation of British Herpetologists
www.F-B-H.co.uk

FroggieB Dragons (mountain horned dragons)
http://www.froggieb.com/MHDHome.html

Herp Station
http://www.petstation.com/herps.html

Kingsnake.com
http://www.kingsnake.com

Leafy Greens Council
www.leafy-greens.org

Melissa Kaplan's Herp Care Collection: Sailfin Dragons
http://www.anapsid.org/sailfin.html

Melissa Kaplan's Herp Care Collection: Water Dragons
http://www.anapsid.org/waterdragons.html

Reptile Forums
http://reptileforums.com/forums/

Reptile Rooms, The
http://www.reptilerooms.org

Robyn's Sailfin Lizard Page
http://www.fishpondinfo.com/sailfin.htm

MAGAZINES

Herp Digest
www.herpdigest.org

Reptiles Magazine
P.O. Box 6050
Mission Viejo, CA 92690
www.animalnetwork.com/reptiles

Reptilia Magazine
Salvador Mundi 2
Spain-08017 Barcelona
Subscripciones-subscriptions@reptilia.org

Photo Credits:

Olivier Antonini: 55, 99, 101, 102
Marion Bacon: 3, 8, 94, and front cover
R. D. Bartlett: 1, 52, 106, 112
Allen Both: 26, 75, 86, 104
Merryl Brackstone (courtesy of Shutterstock): 78
Jim Bridges: 108
Matthwe Campbell: 28
Troy Cassell (courtesy of Shutterstock): 34 and back cover
Scott Corning: 96, 98
Angela Davis (courtesy of Shutterstock): 80

Isabelle Francais: 14, 72
Paul Freed: 66, 76
U. E. Friese: 38, 46, 58
Zoë Funnell (courtesy of Shutterstock): 22, 87
James E. Gerholdt: 15
V. T. Jirousek: 50, 65
Wayne Raymond Johnson: 24, 83
Bert Langerwerf: 29, 30, 36, 40, 44, 49, 91, 114
W. P. Mara: 4, 53
Christian McCarty (courtesy of Shutterstock): 13, 92
Sean McKeown: 68
Roger E. Moore: 57

Aaron Norman: 20, 105, 113
M. P. and C. Piednoir: 33
Patrick Prevost: 42
Wayne Rogers: 17, 60
Mark Smith: 103
Robert G. Sprackland: 37
K. H. Switak: 110, 115
Zoltan Takacs: 63
Kirill Troitsky (courtesy of Shutterstock): 70
John Tyson: 10,
R. W. Van Devender
Zaporozhchenko Yury (courtesy of Shutterstock): 84
David Zoffer: 18, 69

Acanthosaura sp. (mountain horned dragons), 103–105, **103**, **104**, **105**
  A. armata in, 103–104, **103**
  A. capra in, 104, **104**
  A. crucigera in, 104–105
  A. lepidogaster in, 105
acclimation of new water dragons, 14
acrodonts, 7
adults for sale, 13
Agamidae family, 7
aggression, 69–71
Amphibolurinae subfamily, 7
angle-headed dragons. See *Gonocephalus* sp.
appetite loss, 17
Asia, 7, 60
Australia and the water dragons, 5–6, 7, 11, 80
Australian water dragons. See *Physignathus leseurii leseurii; P. l. howitti*

Basiliscus vittatus (basilisk lizard), 114
black soldier flies as food, 41–42
blisters, 53–54, **53**
body shape and size, 62–63, 83–84
breeding, 87
  aggression and, 69–71
  egg binding (dystocia) and, 57
  egg numbers laid following, 90, 91
  egg size and shape in, 72–73
  environmental conditions for, 71
  hatchlings and hatchling care following, 76–77, 92–93
  humidity levels (wet/dry seasons) and, 71
  Hydrosaurus sp. (sailfin dragons) and, 101–102
  incubation period of and temperatures for eggs following, 69, 73–76, 91–92
  nesting behaviors and, 71–73
  outdoor terraria for, 32
  sexing water dragons for, 13, 67–68
  social behavior and, 69–71
  sperm retention by females in, 74
  temperature-dependent sex determination (TDST) and, 73, 89–90
  temperature requirements for, 71, 87, 89
Burma, 60

calcium requirements, 55
Cambodia, 60
captive-bred vs. wild-caught, 9, 10–12
China, 60
climate of natural water dragons range, 61–62, 61t, 81–83, 82t
climbing space, 20
coccidia, 10
cockroaches (six-spotted) as food, 47–48, **49**
coloration of water dragons, 64–65, 84–85
cost of water dragons, 10, 11
crest, **65**
crickets as food, 43–45

diet. See feeding
dorsal scales, 64
dragon agama. See *Japalura splendida*
dystocia (egg binding), 57

earthworms and nightcrawlers as food, 42
egg binding (dystocia), 57
eggs, **91**
  hatchlings and hatchling care following, 76–77, 92–93
  incubation period of and temperature for, 69, 73–76, 91–92
  numbers of, in typical clutch, 90, 91
  size and shape in, 72–73

feeding, 39–49
  black soldier flies in, 41–42
  calcium requirements and, 55
  cockroaches (six-spotted) in, 47–48, **49**
  crickets in, 43–45
  earthworms and nightcrawlers in, 42
  encouraging, 17
  force feeding and, 17

gut-loading and, 47
Hydrosaurus sp. (sailfin dragons) and, 100
insects in, 39–40, 41–43, 65–67, 85–86
lettuce in, caution about, 101
natural diet of, 65–67, 85–86
new arrivals and, 16–17
nutritional content of, insects vs. worms, 43t
rodents in, 48
seasonal variations in, 16
size of food in, 48–49
superworms in, 45–46
temperature effects on, 16
termites in, **44**
vegetable matter in, 39–40, 65–67, 85–86
vitamin A deficiency and, 54
water requirements and, 21–22
flagellates, 10
flies as food, 41–42
Floricke, K., 5
force feeding, 17
forest dragons. See *Hypsilurus* sp.

genus names, 6
Germany and the water dragons, 6
Gonocephalus sp. (angle-headed dragons), 105–109,
105–**109**
G. *bellii*, 106
G. *borneensis*, 106–107
G. *chamaeleontinus*, 107
G. *doriae*, 107, **106**
G. *grandis*, 108, **108**
G. *kuhlii*, 108
G. *lacunosus*, 108
G. *liogaster*, 109
green water dragon. See *Physignathus cocincinus*
greenhouses as enclosures, 35–37
growth and development of hatchlings, 77
Guangdong province, 60
Guangsi province, 60
gut-loading, 47

habitat of the water dragons, 60, 81
handling your water dragons, 56
hatchlings and hatchling care, 76–77, 92–93
growth and development of, 77
humidity levels and, 77
light requirements for, 77

temperature requirements for, 77
health issues, 51–57
appetite loss, 17
blisters in, 53–54, **53**
calcium requirements and, 55
egg binding (dystocia) and, 57
heat stress and, 56–57
injuries in, 56
internal parasites in, 10
metabolic bone disease (MBD) and, 55
nose bouncers and, 55–56, **55**
shedding difficulty in, 52
signs of good health and, 10, 11
skin problems in, 52–53
unhealthy signs in, 54
veterinary selection for, 52, 53
vitamin A deficiency and, 54
heat stress, 56–57
hibernation, 88
hiding areas in enclosures, 27
housing, 19–37. See also outdoor terraria
acclimating new water dragons to, 14
breeding and, 32
climbing space for, 20
greenhouses as, 35–37
hiding areas in, 27
humidity levels in, 15, 26–27
Hydrosaurus sp. (sailfin dragons) and, 99–100
lighting requirements and, 14, 21, 22, 23–26,
24, 37
materials used in, 21
nesting behaviors and, 71–73
outdoor terraria for. See outdoor terraria
plants in, **26**, 28–29, 32
quarantine of new animals and, 15–16
size of, 20
temperature requirements for, 14–15, 22–23
water sources in, 21–22
humidity levels, 15, 26–27
breeding and, wet/dry seasons and, 71
hatchlings and, 77
Hydrosaurus sp. (sailfin dragons) and, 99
Hydrosaurinae, 7
Hydrosaurus sp. (sailfin dragons), 80, 96–102,
96–**102**
breeding of, 101–102
climate of natural environment of, 99

description, appearance of, 97–98
feeding, 100–101
habitat and habits of, 98–99
species confusion surrounding, 96–97
terrarium requirements for, 99–100
Hypsilurus sp. (forest dragons), 80, 109–111
  H. boydii, 109
  H. dilophus, 110
  H. godeffroyi, 110, **110**
  H. spinipes, 111

importation of water dragons, 11–12
incubation period of and temperature for eggs, 69,
  73–76, 91–92
Indochina, 60
Indonesia, 7
infralabial scales, 64
injuries, 56
insects as food, 39–40, 41–43, 65–67, 85–86
internal parasites, 10

Japalura sp. (mountain lizards), 111–114, 112–**114**
Japalura splendida (dragon agama), 112–114, **114**

Klingelhoffer, W., 5–6

Laos, 60
laws and regulations concerning water dragons, 9,
  111
lettuce as food, 101
light requirements, 14, 21, 22, 23–26, **24**, 37
  hatchlings and, 77
  hibernation and, 88
  ultraviolet, 14, 21, 22, 23–26, **24**, 37
Lophognathus sp. (striped water dragons), 7, 114–117
  confusion among species of, 112
  L. gilberti, **116**
  L. longirostris, 114
  L. maculilabris, 114, 115
  L. temporalis, 114, **115**, 116–117
  name change of, 117

Malayan Peninsula, 7
materials used in enclosures, 21
metabolic bone disease (MBD), 55
mountain horned dragons. See *Acanthosaura sp.*
Myanmar, 60

names for water dragons, 7
nesting behaviors, 71–73
New Guinea, 7, 80
Nietzke, 7
nose, 63
nose bouncers, 55–56, **55**
nuchal crest, 63
nutritional content of insects vs. worms, 43t

outdoor terraria, 29–37, **29**. See also housing
  breeding and, 32
  construction of, 29–31, 32
  cover for, 32
  plants in, 32
  temperature variations in, 33
  water sources for, 33–35, 33

parasites, 10
personality and temperament, 107
pet stores, 12–13
Physignathus cocincinus (green water dragons), 6, 7,
  59–77
  breeding habits of, 69–76
  climate of, 61–62, 61t
  coloration of, 64–65
  diet of, in nature, 65–67
  habitat of, 60
  hatchlings of, care of, 76–77
  nesting behaviors in, 71–73
  range of, 60
  sexing of, 67–68
  size and body shape of, 62–63
  social behaviors of, 69–71
Physignathus leseurii leseurii; P. l. howitti (Australian water
  dragons), 79–93, **78**, **80**
  breeding habits of, 87
  climate of, 81–83, 82t
  coloration of water dragons, 84–85
  description, appearance of, 83–85
  diet of, in nature, 85–86
  habitat of, 81
  hatchlings of, care of, 92–93
  hibernation of, indoor, 88
  range of, 80–81
  size and body shape of, 83–84
Physignathus mentager, 7
plants, in enclosures, **26**, 28–29, 32

postrostral scales, 64
purchasing your water dragons, 9–17
    acclimation of new water dragons and, 14
    adults for, 13
    best time for, 9
    cost of, 10, 11
    feeding the new arrival following, 16–17
    healthy animals for, 10, 11
    imported animals and, 11–12
    pet stores for, 12–13
    quarantine of new animals after, 15–16

quarantine of new animals, 15–16

range of water dragons, 60, 80–81
reproduction. See breeding
Reptiles and Amphibians from Foreign Countries, 5
rodents as food, 48
rostral scales, 63, 64

sailfin dragons. See Hydrasaurus sp.
sailfin lizard, **46**
scales, 63, 64
scientific names, 6
seasonal feeding variations, 16
sexing water dragons, 13, 67–68
    temperature-dependent sex determination
        (TDST) and, 73, 89–90
shedding difficulty, 52
signs of good health in water dragons, 10, 11
size of water dragons, 62, 83–84
size of enclosure for, 20, 100
size of food, 48–49
skin problems, 52–53
    blisters in, 53–54, **53**
    shedding difficulty in, 52
snout-to-vent length (SVL), 62
social behavior, 69–71
South Africa, 11
species names, 6
sperm retention by females, 74
spines, 63
striped water dragons. See Lophognathus sp.
subcaudal scales, 64

subocular scales, 64
subspecies, 6
superworms as food, 45–46
supralabial scales, 64
SVL. See snout-to-vent length

taxonomy, 7–8
tegu lizards, 40
temperature-dependent sex determination (TDST),
    73, 89–90
temperature requirements, 14–15, 22–23
    breeding and, 71, 87, 89
    climate of natural water dragons range and,
        61–62, 61t, 81–83, 82t
    egg incubation and, 69, 73–76, 91–92
    feeding and, 16
    greenhouses and, 35–37
    hatchlings and, 77
    heat stress and, 56–57
    hibernation and, 88
    Hydrosaurus sp. (sailfin dragons) and, 99
    outdoor terraria and, 33
    temperature-dependent sex determination
        (TDST) and, 73, 89–90
    thermometers and, 23
termites as food, **44**
Thailand, 11, 60
thermometers, 23

ultraviolet light requirements, 14, 21, 22, 23–26,
    24, 37
unhealthy signs in a water dragons, 54

vegetable matter as food, 39–40, 65–67, 85–86
ventral scales, 64
veterinary selection, 52, 53
Vietnam, 10, 59, 60, 65
vitamin A deficiency, 54

water sources, in enclosures, 21–22, 60–61
    outdoor terraria, 33–35
wild-caught vs. captive-bred, 9, 10–12

Yunnan province, 60